Golden City

The wind, the wind, the wind blows high
The snow comes falling from the sky:
Maisie Drummond says she'll die
For the want of the golden city.

She is handsome, she is pretty
She is the girl of the golden city:
She is handsome, one two three
Come and tell me who shall be!

Golden City

Scottish Children's Street Games & Songs

James T. R. Ritchie

MERCAT PRESS
EDINBURGH

First published in 1965 by Oliver and Boyd
Reprinted 1999 by Mercat Press
James Thin, 53 South Bridge, Edinburgh EH1 1YS
© Margaret Longstaff and Adrian Pearce, 1999

ISBN 1873644 973

Printed and bound in Great Britain by Redwood Books

CONTENTS

INTRODUCTION

Coming to Edinburgh from 'down south' to take the enviable job of Keeper at the Museum of Childhood, I discovered in the office library Dr Ritchie's books *The Singing Street* and *Golden City*. I could have found no better introduction to the flavour of past childhoods in Edinburgh. Reading about peevers, peeries and bools was a revelation. If new names, they were also delightfully familiar games. I played ollies (bools, or otherwise known as marbles), tick (in Edinburgh tig) and watched my sister play hopscotch (peevers or beds). My niece in Birmingham told me skipping rhymes in another accent but not very different to those chanted by Edinburgh girls thirty years before. It was wonderful to find these games particular and yet so universal.

The books, particularly *Golden City*, are now well thumbed and flagged with slips of paper marked, Ballie, Dusting Bluebells, Semolina—a game you played in the tenement stair, and so on. They have served well over the years, invaluable in giving answers to teachers, students and activity workers from all over the world interested in games children used to play. Quoting from the books in talks the museum staff give has invariably released other treasured if half-forgotten memories of skipping or counting-out rhymes that in turn trigger fond or thought-provoking memories of 'when we were young'. Many elderly ladies have impressed us in demonstrating their never-lost skill with the Diabolo.

Dr Ritchie and his talented and enthusiastic colleagues Nigel McIsaac and Raymond Townsend who formed the Norton Park Group in the 1950s kindly allowed us to show and sell in the museum their film *The Singing Street*. Some of the games recorded in *Golden City* appear in the film. Against the background of a smoky Edinburgh and Leith without bumper to bumper traffic, with the children in sensible cardigans, blazers and overcoats, the film has charmed and fascinated the many thousands of visitors to the museum. It shows scenes remote yet recognisable. John Grierson, the famous documentary film maker, wrote that it was 'the best amateur film I ever saw… The reason for it being wonderful was quite simple. Somebody loved something and conveyed it.'

In this book, the children's world Dr Ritchie captured is in many ways a bygone era. Children appeared to play safely outside in the street unsupervised, the television had not the hold over everyone's attention, a shadow of post-war austerity still lingered and not all games needed batteries or computer chips. Families seemed to stay in one place for longer, allowing children to form more stable groups of playmates for friendships to develop, the younger ones learning the games, rhymes and chants from their admired elders. We suspect that the tradition and evolution of these games has been interrupted. Children now take part in a much wider range of activities, ballet and karate classes replace just going out to play. Even the sometimes eventful walk to and from school is being replaced by the school run in the car. All good progress and showing parental concern for the child's welfare, but I wonder if the group games that children used to play when there was nothing else to do, did not help cement friendships and let them act out wishes, fears and fantasies in self-organised games with self-enforced rules.

I guess and hope that some of these games still go on in the school playground, if not in car-lined streets, with words no doubt changed to fit today's world; little-known because they are part of the child's own world, not for grown-ups to see. Let us hope there will be others who will gain the children's trust and with wit, sensitivity and foresight, record these games for posterity as Jim Ritchie did with this excellent collection that it is so good to see back in print.

John Heyes
Museum of Childhood, Edinburgh
September 1999

PROLOGUE

Thirty years ago when I first started out as a teacher I found myself appointed to a school which stood on the borders between the city of Edinburgh and the port of Leith. In fact I was assured that the boundary line actually ran right through the school, so that although my science laboratory was in Leith, many of the other rooms, including the room in which I taught mathematics, lay in Edinburgh.

Sometime before, I'd bought at a second-hand book-stall a copy of Robert Chambers' *Popular Rhymes of Scotland* (1841). This famous and most original collection is devoted to what the author called "the natural literature" of Scotland. It greatly interested me and I assumed (as its preface suggested) that this natural literature was a thing of the past. Then another book came my way. The writer and novelist Norman Douglas brought out the second edition of his *London Street Games* (1931). This slim volume, first printed in 1916, proved that traditional rhymesters were still active. I began to remember many of the rhymes of my own day, and I got the notion of collecting newer ones. But I wondered how this might be done. I didn't fancy very much the idea of going round the streets, notebook in hand!

One morning in Norton Park School, I was teaching science in Leith, and finding the response on this occasion not very lively, I asked: "Then what do you like doing?" The class answered: "We like playing games." "What games?" They told me, and I began there and then to write them down. In the afternoon, whilst teaching mathematics in Edinburgh, I also found time to jot down some more games. From then on I collected every sort of rhyme or playing jingle, and my collection grew.

After the War I put together a radio programme named *The Singing Street*. This was broadcast on the Scottish Home Service in 1949. Several more programmes with the same title followed; and in 1951, in association with two of my colleagues in the school, a film called *The Singing Street* was made. No one before had ever thought either of recording the singing games of children or of making a film of them. A booklet of the rhymes and songs used in the film was issued, and this was the first publication in Great Britain which showed that the children of this island had made poetry out of modern life, and unlike many grown-ups were actually living in the twentieth century.

The rhymes I'd been collecting (as I very soon realised) didn't belong to Edinburgh (or Leith) alone. They were universal, and the different cities in Scotland, England, Ireland and Wales all possessed and seemed to prefer their own variations. I made it a rule never to take any rhymes out of any book, only to note down what I heard by word of mouth, and from the pupils of this one school.

Last year some of this material was published in *The Singing Street*. It was the strongly held opinion of D. H. Lawrence that Edinburgh was "more of a true city than any town England ever produced". In *The Singing Street,* through a variety of rhymes, nicknames, songs and sayings, this independent and thoroughly urban character (first established by the Makars) is shown to be kept alive, not only by the children in the street and the family round the fireside, but also by the many students and football followers.

The present book, *Golden City,* is wholly taken up with Edinburgh children at play. But every city up and down the country must recognise and enjoy the games that are described here.

The youngsters in the Scottish capital play chiefly in three places: the street, the back-green, and the school playground. The playground is so rich in wit and humour that "The Bell, the Bell, the Bumbee Bell", the chapter dealing with it, turned out to be too big for inclusion. It is hoped that this will be published later in a smaller volume.

James T. R. Ritchie,
1965

1

PLAYING IN THE GREEN

Most Edinburgh children make their first venture alone into the world through the "backie" or back-green; and in a working-class district in the bad old days of overcrowding, all that was green about the green was its name. Usually it was beaten into a hard, greyish-brown mass, with grass growing only at the sides or in the untrodden corners. The first tune a beginner picks out on the piano is almost certain to be:

The Sailor's Shirt
- ✧ Oh, I can wash a sailor's shirt
  Oh, I can wash it clean
  Oh, I can wash a sailor's shirt
  And hang it in the green!

Long ago, instead of "hang it in" the words were "bleach it on" and bleaching is much more possible nowadays for in many of the old back-greens the grass has now returned. There isn't such a density of stamping feet! Legally the green is set aside for drying clothes, and many children meet with difficulties playing there if some neighbour insists on the letter of the law.

- ✧ "We cannie play in oor back-green cause o' the fleurs."

- ✧ "This wife, she used to get seik [sick] o' us, me and ma two big brothers aye runnin' past her windie intae the green, she wrote a letter tae the man that owns the hoose, the architect I think, and he come doun and tellt ma ma no to let us play in the back-green for it was for washin' only."

- ✧ "The folk in the first flett [flat] chucked a bucket o' water at us and the bucket an' a'."

- ✧ "Oor back-green's a stanie backie and when A [I] was nine, A smashed three windies playin' tennis."

✧ "Dae you think this is fair? We were playin' fitba' in the green and A burst a windie and we had tae pey [pay] for it and they gote it through the insurance."

✧ "A keep a tortoise and we went roond tae the backie an' we were gettin' gress for the tortoise an' we let it go for a meenit [minute] an' doun come the wife fae [from] the stair an' she come across wi' a bag and paper an' she started hittin' us an' she nearly stood on ma tortoise an' A say'd 'Get oaf the tortoise' an' she say'd 'Dinnie be sae saucy', an' a laddie say'd 'Dae ye mean ketchup?'—and then we hudtie [had to] skedaddle."

Factories[1] of every description hem in many of the back-greens and this leads to a lot of climbing and scrambling over roofs for "dowsed ba's [balls that have gone out of bounds]." A good many tenement stairways have mezzanine floors and very often a laddie's earliest ambition is "to dreep the first-flett windie," that is, drop to the ground from the lowest half-flat window.

The railings that used to bound most of the back-greens were scrapped during the Second World War so that "gettin' spiked" is now uncommon. But the walls remain; and walking their high tops or "dreepin' " them is still an exciting pastime. A youngster who wants some assistance in clambering over a wall cries "Gies [give us] a hyst [hoist]!" or "Gies a dookie!"[2] A "basket" means standing on someone's clasped hands; and a "backie" or "buckie" means standing on someone's shoulders. A dookie used to mean getting on to the back of "a pal who dooked doun [ducked down]." Nowadays a dookie can mean any kind of helping hand; and it is the favourite term.

It's in the green that the boys first learn to play "bools [marbles]"; and the girls to dance their first ring games. And "skipping," "chasie," "hide-and-seek," the different "tigs" and

[1] The tenement-factory conglomeration produced by accident a playing environment of exciting variety: and unless present-day architecture incorporates such ideas, it's dead from the start. The houses in modern schemes are so dull and unmysterious. They have no "Unknown Corners" such as haunted painters like James Pryde (1866-1941). Parks are always placed far too far away from where the children live.

[2] "My cousin in Irvine, Ayrshire, uses the word 'puntie' for 'dookie'."

a multitude of other games are begun in this setting. And here too, the bigger girls (from twelve to fourteen) are pretty expert in amusing or pacifying their smaller brothers and sisters:

Wee Johnny Nory

❖ I'll tell ye a story
Aboot wee Johnny Nory
He climbed up a stair
And he fell doun a storey.

❖ I'll tell ye a story
About wee Johnny Nory
Three steps up
And a wee wee doorie.

❖ I'll tell ye a story
About wee Johnny Nory
And now my story has begun:
I'll tell ye another
About wee Johnny's brother
And now my story is done.

❖ "Wheesht!
I'll tell ye a story
About wee Johnny Nory
If ye dinnie speak in the middle o' it.
Will ye no?"

"No."

"Aw, ye've spoke [spoken] in the middle o' it."

Another story-telling joke goes as follows:

A Hundred Stories

❖ "Would you like to hear a hundred stories?"

"Aye."

"Well, here's the first:

Judy and Shurrup ran a race
Judy stopped to tie her lace
Whae won?"

"Shurrup!"

"Oh, in that case I'm no gaun to tell ye ma hundred stories."

A Song

✧ Tell me a story
Tell me a story
Tell me a story before I go to bed
Tell me about the bumble bees
Tell me about your clarty knees
Tell me a story before I go to bed.

Eye Nose . . .

✧ Eye nose cheekie cheekie chin
Cheekie cheekie chin knows I!

A baby or very young child is greeted and lightly touched as these words are repeated:

An older rhyme of the same kind is:

Chin Chin Cherry

✧ Chin chin cherry
Mou' mou' merry
Cheek cheek chebby
Nose nose nebby
Eye eye winky
Broo broo blinky
Over the hills and far away!

You begin with the chin and finally brush your hand gently over the "bairn's heid." Another version starts the other way:

Broo broo brunty . . .

and you finish under the chin with the words and action of:
Chuck-a-pudden, chuck-a-pudden, chuck-a-pudden!

If a child stumbles or accidentally or deliberately knocks something over this rhyme is used:

Annie Bananie

✧ Ann-ie Banan-ie,
What do you think o' that?
She *up*-sets the table
And nearly kills the cat!

The cat began to bubble,
She hit it wi' the shovel:
Ann-ie Banan-ie,
What do you think o' that?

✧ "I like looking efter wee bairns but no ma niece or that! A hammer thaim."

✧ "I noticed ma wee sister, she puts her hands over her eyes and she says, 'Ha, ha, ha, ye cannie see me!' and ye see, she thinks if she cannie see you, you cannie see her!'"

Before the 1920s most children would call an elder brother their "big billie" and a smaller one their "wee billie." Since then, American expressions like "kid sister" and "kid brother" have been supplanting our older and kindlier Scots. "Ma brother" is often shortened to "ma bra'." And this primitive custom still lingers on:

✧ "You cut yoursel' on the back o' the wrist or on a finger, and your pal does the same, and ye jine [join] the cuts thegither so that the blood mixes and efter that ye're *blood brothers*. It took us ages to cut oorsel's, we were that feared. Usually the idea o' daein' it starts when somebody cuts theirsel' by accident."

Numerous plays and ploys which serve to entertain the very young bring in and make a clever use of the hands and fingers:

Guessing Hands
✧ Nivvie, nivvie, nick nack,
Which hand will ye tak?
Take the richt or take the wrang
I'll beguile ye if I can.

Clap-Handies
✧ Clap clap handies
Clap clap away:
This is the way we exercise
Upon a rainy day.

The rain is falling very fast
We can't get out to play
So this is the way we exercise
Upon a rainy day.

✧ Clap-a-clap-a-handies
Mammie's at the well[3]
Daddie's away to London
To buy wee baby a bell.

[3] Or "Mammie's no well."

Interlocking, Wagging & Rocking Fingers

✧   There's your mother's knives and forks
There's your mother's table
There's your granny's looking-glass
And there's your baby's cradle:

Rock, rock, rumply Jock
We'll a' get up at ten o'clock
Ten o'clock's owre *ª*soon   *ª* pron. *sin*
We'll a' get up in the *ᵇ*afternoon.   *ᵇ* pron. *efternin*

✧   There's the church
There's the steeple
Open the doors
And see a' the people!

Here's the choir-boys
Going upstairs
And this is the minister
Saying his prayers!

There are many other games which children play with their fingers:

One Two Three Four Five

✧   One two three four five
Can you catch a fish alive?
Why did you let it go?
Because it bit my finger so.

"Ye do it wi' a bairn. As ye say the rhyme, ye grip each o' its fingers in turn, no hard, and ye try to finish so that when ye come to 'so', ye squeeze its pinkie—jist a wee bit harder—that's the bite!"

Incy Wincy Spider

✧   Incy wincy spider
Climbing up the spout:
Down came the rain
And washed the spider out.

Out came the sunshine
Dried up all the rain:
Incy wincy spider
Climbed the spout again.

The forefinger of one hand is placed on the thumb of the other and the thumb of this hand on the forefinger of the other. With the topmost touching fingers as centre, the lower fingers keep swivelling round and so the spider climbing up or down is simulated.

Two Little Dicky-Birds

✧ Two little dicky-birds
Sitting on a wall:
One named Peter
One named Paul:

Fly away Peter
Fly away Paul:
Come back Peter
Come back Paul!

"Peter" and "Paul" (each a small piece of paper) are stuck to the nails of the two forefingers, and these "birds" apparently fly away because the bare second fingers deceptively take their places. Reversing this procedure "Peter" and "Paul" return.

Round & Round the Garden

✧ Round and round the garden
I lost my Teddy Bear:
One step, two step,
And tickle you up there!

First two lines are played with the forefinger on the child's palm, the third line on the forearm, and the last under the arm.

This Wee Piggy

✧ This wee piggy went to the market
This wee piggy stayed at hame
This wee piggy got bread and cheese
And this wee piggy got nane
And this wee piggy cried "Wee wee wee!"
A' the ᵃwey hame.   ᵃ *way*

Do this After Me

✧ After saying "Do this after me" someone proceeds to touch one finger point after another starting at the little finger and going back to it while chanting "Tom tom tom tom *woops*

B

tom *woops* tom tom tom tom." "Tom" is said for each finger, and "*woops*" for the valley between the forefinger and thumb. Few repeat this successfully, because they fail to observe that this rigmarole ends with the player *folding her arms.*

Don't Touch the Baby

❖ With the forefinger of one hand, a girl touches the top of every finger of her other hand—with the exception of the little finger. As she does so she keeps on saying:

> Mother says, "Don't touch the baby!"
> Father says, "Don't touch the baby!"
> Sister says, "Don't touch the baby!"
> Brother says, "Don't touch the baby!"

The person who doesn't know the trick usually asks, "Which is the baby?" The girl then holds out the little finger in such a way that the questioner grips it, only to be indignantly told, "Don't touch the baby!"

If You had a Baby

❖ You seize some one's pinkie [little finger] and bend it back, while at the same time you ask, "If you had a baby what would you call it?" And the owner of the pinkie can't help from squealing "Ah-h!"

Skipping is as much a back-green sport as it is a street or playground one. Here's a song for skipping, or for a ballie, or for amusing the smaller folk:

Keep the Sunny Side Up

❖ Keep the sunny side up up
> [*Ye lift your right leg.*
> Keep the sunny side up up.
> [*Ye lift up your other leg.*
>
> See them soldiers marching on
> [*Ye march.*
> And Cliff Richard sing a song.
> [*Pretend to play a guitar.*
>
> Touch your toes, be an Eskimo
> Touch your knees, be a Japanese.

The tune is called *Sunny Side Up*; and after the last line you go back to the beginning.

Swinging and turning somersaults are also much indulged in:
Here are two songs that have to do with swinging.

Rub-a-Dub-Dub

❖ Rub-a-dub-dub
Three men in a tub
And who do you think they are?

The butcher, the baker,
The candlestick-maker,
They all went to the Fair.

They went to Marshall's garden
And there they found a farthing:
They gave it to their mother
To buy a baby brother.

The brother was so cross
That they bought a lily-white horse:
With a high *a*swee and a low swee   *aswing*
And a swee to let the cat *b*die.   *b*pron. *dee*

To begin with, this is chanted, and singing starts on the line
"They all went to the Fair." "A swee to let the cat die" means
bringing the swing to a dead stop. Other versions add the
couplet:

The horse gave a squeal
And down came the wheel.

And in place of "baby brother" we get "little brother" or
"Irish brother," and very often this ending:

A high swing, a low swing,
And off you come
Wi' a *a*skelp on the bum   *aslap*
Wi' a red-hot poker!

A Swing for Sale

❖ A swing for sale
A monkey's tail
If ye take it
Ye'll get the jail.

❖ A swing for sale
A fairy-tale
And if you want it
You go to jail.

"If ye were in the Swing Park, and ye were gaun [going] away hame [home], you would sing that song for to give your swing away to somebody else. Laddies often yell: 'A swing for sale! A swing for sale!' But when somebody else goes to get the swing, they've only been pretending, for then they cry out: 'A monkey sale!'"

The city Swing Parks have drawn many of the children away from their cramped greens. In the new quarters plenty of new games have been devised; on the merry-go-round ("Blindie Tig") and on the chute ("Trains"). Naturally the swings are the greatest attraction.

Bucking Broncos

∻ "A laddie's maybe sitting on the seat o' a swing and you ask him 'Do you want a bronco?' and you stand up on the seat in front o' him, and ye beam him up and up, and then at the last minute, ye jump off and ye must run under the seat and his legs that are danglin' doun. At the same time he 'bucks [jerks up]'."

American Broncos, or Chinese Bronchos, or Frenchies

∻ "Ye're jist yoursel' on the swing, stannin', and ye beam up until at the very last minute ye kick the seat owre [over] your heid as ye let go the chains wi' your hands. And the chains go into a knot. Then ye dae it again and they go into a second knot. Ye can have a pal on a swing alongside o' ye and ye can have a contest to see who can get the maist knots in their swing."

∻ "If naebody's in the Swing Park ye play at Chinese Broncos yoursel' an' sometimes ye put the swing right owre [over] the bar. If ye're co't ye're taken to the cops."

∻ "At night if it's still light and ye dinnie want the swings to be locked up, ye wrap them right roond the bar, and ye slink back later and get them doun, for the Parkie's usually an auld man and he cannie climb the poles."

A "Tarzan Swing" is a single rope hanging from the branch of a tree. The sport of Tarzan-swinging isn't practical in the back-greens; it's much more often enjoyed on the woodland edges of public parks—out of sight of the "Parkie [park-keeper]."

- "There's yin [one] behind the maltings. Ye swing right out and ye drop off."

- "In the woods at Portie [Portobello] one boy fell and killed hissel'."

- "There's one at Puddocky that swings across the water and back."

And here is a song for a somersault:

Wash the Dishes

- Wash the dishes
  Dry the dishes
  Turn the dishes
  Over!

Two girls join hands round a third girl. As the first two lines are recited, their clasped hands tilt first to one side, then to the other, and on the third line the girl in the middle is made to turn a somersault.

It is also in the back-green that many children first learn to recognise the few birds, the one or two creepie-crawlies, and the handful of flowers that they know. The king of city birds is the sparrow—which in Scots is variously called "sparrie," "speug," or "spadger:"

- In the Trinity district our name for a sparrow was a "spurdie."

    Who killed Cock Robin?
    "I", said the Spadger,
    "With my bow and adger,[4]
    I killed Cock Robin!"

The "stuckie [starling]" is a persistent rooster, and an occasional nester. Other birds are known chiefly through such beliefs as that

- "If ye cut a jackdaw's tongue wi' a threepenny-bit, it can learn to speak—ma cousin in the country tellt me."

But "blackies [blackbirds]" and "mavies [thrushes]" are not unknown.

[4] Or "With my tallywadger."

"Rats' tails [plantains]" and "pee-the-beds [dandelions]" are the commonest flowers growing in the back-green. To almost every umbelliferous plant (all so like hemlock) city children attach the name "dead man's florry" (or "flourish"). They have a better memory for what's eatable such as "nippy biscuits [nasturtium leaves]" or for mischievous plants like "Stickie Willie."

Making daisy-chains is still a children's amusement in the summer parks; and "Does 'ou like butter?"—a liking proved by the golden reflexion that appears when a buttercup is held under your chin—is still a question that's asked.

"Clipshears [earwigs]" are abhorred, and so are "cloakers [beetles]," which you never stand on, or there'll be rain. Spiders are never killed either.

✦   In the country I saw a spider wi' a white back. I killed it and it started to rain. I hut [hit] it owre [over] the heid [head] three times wi' the mallet. We were in a tent. And there were black beetles. Ye should have seen one. It took me nine hits to kill it. It didnie [didn't] half rain!"

A good many boys either keep or have kept "doos [pigeons]," and therefore are well acquainted with "horsemen" or "hawkers" and their "blaws:"

✦   "A 'horseman' is a big burd wi' a big chist and it sits wi' its heid [head] back and its chist right out. It can be either a doo [dove] or a hen. When it's flying it makes a skelping noise for its wings hit at the top. There's a man near me has a black-tip doo wi' a white bib and ma horseman would vee right doun to it and show to it—that is, if it was rampin'."

✦   "A horseman brings in other hens and doos and ye keep them and sell them—that's the game!"

Many of these young pigeon-fanciers go after "crowp [loft-less pigeons]" in other ways. They tempt the doves to alight by sprinkling some maize on the pavement. The maize lies in a loop of string which is eventually pulled to catch the birds by the legs. Another enterprise is to collect "squeaks [young pigeons]" from the nesting-places which swarm under railway bridges.

And here are some of the troubles and trials of youngsters "in the fancy:"

❖   "We still have the tummler. We've sellt him twice and he aye comes back to us. We still have the mealie hen and the silver hen. An' the white fantail and the red doo [dove]—she cannie [can't] fly. She hut [hit] the telegraph wires. But she'll be a' right when she gets her flights back, her three best feathers. One doo we bought flew straight away and she never even looked back!"

❖   "They're complainin' aboot us using the single end.[5] They say people should be living in it, no pigeons. It's a middle flat but there's wa'er in it, dreepin' fae [from] the ceilin'. It's been empie for ages. The last folk to bide there was a man, a woman, three laddies, and a dug. An Alsatian. Ronnie and me went in and we sawed the windie in half. We hud tae [had to]! We widnie [wouldn't] have got the dookit [dovecot] oot!"

There are many other diversions that children can enjoy in the back-green. "Howkin' [digging] holes" is one:

❖   "Have ye ever seen a green dug [dog]?"
       "Naw!"
       "Ye've never seen a green bein' dug!"

Another is "lighting fires," that everybody "coories roond [huddles round]." Then there is "chuckin' yucks or yawkers [throwing stones]." "B'ilin' tatties [boiling potatoes]" over a fire ranks very old as a back-green ploy. It is included by "Glorious Geikie" [6] among the many amusements of his day— the 1820s and the 1830s.

Being so near home the child can call up to his mother and get thrown down to him a "jeelly piece" or a "jammy piece" or "a piece on jam." (A piece of bread is called a "dad o' chuck.")

[5] A house or flat consisting of only one apartment. In the word "single", the "g" isn't hard; it is sung as in "sing."

[6] Walter Geikie (1795-1837) was an artist whose greatest inspiration came from the common street and what the Victorians called "low life" (and which George Moore insisted, "is really the only life"). Geikie's drawings are sometimes rich in wit but most of them are plain, down-right studies—rather like Vincent van Gogh's during his Dutch period.

Anyone who appears in the green holding a very big "piece,"
is likely to be greeted with:

✧ "That's an awfie sair [awfully sore] hand ye have!"

If anyone is "greetin' [weeping]," grown-ups sometimes ask
in the passing, in the sing-song lilt of the Newhaven fishwife:

✧ "Wha stole your tre'cle scone, ma lamb?"

Boys and girls like to play near their own homes. In the
autumn when the laddies go "pinchin' peers," or "knockin'
yapps" or "aipples," even they prefer to raid the back-green
nearest at hand.

✧ "Last night a' ma pals were gettin' pears oot o' the palace, the
   Queen's palace, and they were gie in' them a' away. We jist
   climbed up the wa' and the gress goes doun like that—it's dead
   easy. They shook the trees and the pears came droppin' doun.
   I think they were for King Olaf.[7] A wee white Scottie came
   oot but it never touched us. It kennt better. I'm always guard.
   I'm the best guard, for if anything happens, I'm always away
   furst."

A "back-green concert" is an entertainment got up by
children, usually to aid some deserving cause:

✧ "We would have our concert in No. 9 Rossie Place. It's the
   best green, there's no grass in it, it's nearly all concrete."

✧ "We could have a fancy-dress concert, or a singing concert, or
   plays, such as *Hansel and Gretel*, or *Hot and Cold in All the Rooms*,
   or *Little Red Riding Hood*—we'd put different words to the
   plays, of course, and make them more funny."

✧ "Threepence is what we charge children, sixpence for adults."

✧ "We have tea at the end."

Tap-dancing is a skill that's greatly acclaimed here and the
favourite song for this type of dancing is:

✧   I was walking in the park one day
        In the merry merry month of May

[7] King Olaf of Norway paid a state visit to Edinburgh in October 1962.

I was taken by surprise
By a lovely pair of eyes
I was walking in the park one day
In May!

"Playing at schools" very often takes the form of *Jenny Green*, a traditional back-green play. This little sketch has kept the same pattern and the same old jokes for the last thirty years (1930-60):

JENNY GREEN

Characters, TEACHER, PUPILS, and JENNY GREEN

◇ Scene: "Ye sit on the copestone, or on the stairs, or on the form o' the Swing Park, or on the edge o' the kerb—and ye pretend that's the classroom. The Teacher comes in, but Jenny Green stays outside."

TEACHER [*calling the register*]: Daffie Smith!
DAFFIE SMITH: Present, Miss!
TEACHER: Chrissie Cabbage!
CHRISSIE CABBAGE: Present, Miss!
TEACHER: Teenie Weenie!
TEENIE WEENIE: Present, Miss!
TEACHER: Jenny Green! [*No answer.*] Jenny Green! Jenny Green!
JENNY GREEN: [*skipping in*]: Here I am, Miss.
TEACHER: Where have you been, Jenny?
JENNY GREEN: I've been sitting on my mother's boiler keeping my father's shirt warm.
TEACHER: Well, don't be late again. Now we shall have Geography. Jenny Green!
JENNY GREEN: Yes, Miss.
TEACHER: Say "geography."
JENNY GREEN: Dogs' tails.
TEACHER: Geography!
JENNY GREEN: Dogs' tails!
TEACHER: Geog-ra-phy!
JENNY GREEN: Dogg-ies-tails!
TEACHER: Ach, never mind that! It's time for the milk. [*To* JENNY GREEN] Go and get the milk, and give one to everyone, while I go and see the Headmaster. [TEACHER *and* JENNY *both go out:* JENNY *presently returns, bringing the milk, and goes round the pupils, drinking the milk herself.*]

JENNY GREEN: One to you, and one to you, and one to you.

TEACHER [*coming in*]: Has Jenny given the milk out yet?

CHRISSIE CABBAGE: No, Miss, she said she was keeping them for herself.

TEACHER [*to* JENNY]: Did you drink them all yourself?

JENNY GREEN: No, Miss. [*Pointing*] Ye see that wee hole in the wa'? Well, a wee moose [mouse] come oot and drunk it a'.

TEACHER: Well, I want you now to go for half-a-dozen caramels.

JENNY GREEN: All right, give me the money. [JENNY *goes out, and then comes back tugging at an imaginary rope over her shoulder*]. Will I bring them in, Miss?

TEACHER: Of course, what else would you do?

JENNY [*brings "them" in.*]

TEACHER [*holding up her hands*]: Jenny, what on earth is this? I told you to get caramels, not camels!

JENNY GREEN: Oh, I thoat [thought] ye said camels, Miss.

TEACHER: Go and take them back, and get caramels!

JENNY GREEN [*a little later*]: Here you are, Miss.

TEACHER: Now, you give them out to each girl and don't eat them to yourself, while I go and see the Headmaster. [*She goes out.*]

JENNY GREEN: The teacher told me to share them, but I am eating them all myself. ["*A' the other lassies start to greet.*"]

TEACHER [*coming in*]: Did Jenny Green give out the caramels right?

TEENIE WEENIE: No, Miss, she ate them all herself.

TEACHER: Jenny, what have you to say for yourself now?

JENNY GREEN: It was like this, Miss. [*Pointing*] Do you see that other corner? Well, the cat come oot and ate all the caramels.

TEACHER: Cat! What cat?

JENNY GREEN: Please, Miss, there's the bell for playtime!

From amongst "the pupils" a new Teacher and a new Jenny Green are then picked and the play begins all over again with numerous variations or additions:

JENNY GREEN: I've been sitting on my mother's boiler, keeping my bum warm . . .

TEACHER: Say "History."

JENNY GREEN: Historic.

TEACHER: History!
JENNY GREEN: Historic!
TEACHER: His-to-ry!
JENNY GREEN: His-to-ric!

Or Jenny Green is sent for "hose" and brings back a "horse"; or she's asked to get the "horse" (for gymnastics) and she fetches a "real" horse. Or else the sewing teacher sends her for "needles" and she returns with "beetles."

Any of the many songs known to children can be sung and are sung in the back-green. A few of them are more closely associated with the green than any other place:

> *Bonnie Wee Jeanie*
>
> ✧ Bonnie wee Jeanie
> Nice wee Jeanie
> Bonnie wee Jeanie Shaw:
> What will a' the laddies ^adae   ^a *do*
> When Jeanie gangs awa'?
>
> Some will meet
> And some will ^agreet   ^a *weep*
> And some will run awa':
> That's what a' the laddies'll dae
> When Jeanie gangs awa'!

This is very often sung when some playmate is flitting out of the district.

> *Long Live my Auntie Jean*
>
> ✧ Long live my Auntie Jean
> Long may she sell ice cream
> In oor back-green:
> Fill us a great big cone
> That weighs a half a stone
> Then we will never ever moan
> In oor back-green.

Tune: *The National Anthem.* The second line is sometimes "She lives in Aberdeen." The green (like the street) has a healthy disrespect for both patriotism and party politics. Songs like

Three Cheers for the Red, White and Blue, Land of Hope and Glory,
and *The Red Flag* are dealt with as follows:

- Three cheers for the red, white and blue
  It sticks to your bum like glue . . .

- Land of Dope and Tory . . .

- The people's flag is turning pink . . .

Maggie and Willie

- Oh Maggie's a smasher
  Got a face like a *ᵃtattie-basher*   *ᵃ potato-masher*
  A nose like a *ᵇchippit aipple*   *ᵇ chipped apple*
  And two smelly feet.

  Oh Willie's a smasher
  Got a face like a squashed tomater
  A nose like a pickled onion
  And two smelly feet.

Antonio

- I know Antonio
  He sells ice cream-io
  In our back-green-io
  Thruppence a cone-io . . .

Which is sung to the well-known air:

- La donna mobilé
  My legs are wobble-y
  No bloomin' wonder
  Look what they're under!

Bonnie Jimmie

- I'm going in the train
  You're no coming wi' me
  I've got a *ᵃfellie o' my ain*   *ᵃ fellow*
  And they ca' him Bonnie Jimmie.

  He has a tartan kilt
  He wears it in the fashion
  And every time I see him
  I *ᵃcannie* help *ᵇfae* laughin'.   *ᵃ can't*   *ᵇ from*

Pop Goes the Weasel

✧ Half a pound o' tuppeny rice
Half a pound o' treacle
Mix it up and make it nice—
Pop goes the weasel!

This is danced as well as sung. An alternative third line is: "That's the way the money goes."—And another version runs:

✧ Every night when I go home
Monkey's on the table
Take a stick and knock him off—
Pop goes the weasel!

"A lot o' lassies can play. Everybody takes a partner except one. The partners hold hands and the one that's out, she goes in between them, and then she takes the hands o' the person she's facin' and they sing and dance to the rhyme. Of course the one that's left out now, she goes and breaks up another pair."

O me Goss me Goss me Golly

✧ O me goss me goss me golly
There's a spider on the wallie:
And all the men that dance around me—
O mister gooby gooby gooby goes to ty tum
Me yammie yammie yammie O me I lum
Me yammie yammie yammie O me I.

Have you heard of Ginger Rogers?
Have you heard of Betty Grable?
You never see her face without a smile—
O Mister gooby gooby gooby goes to ty tum
Me yammie yammie yammie O me I lum
Me yammie yammie yammie O me I.

Four girls stand four-square while a fifth mimes and dances up and down the centre, and also round each of the others— rather cheekily and very daintily. This dance belonged to the 1940s. While playing or moving in the green or in the street most children, without being aware of it, are dancing all the time.

Jenny Cock-a-lee

✜ O Jenny ^aCock-a-lee   ^a pron. *Coke-*
Come to bed and cuddle me
I'll ^bgie ye a cup o' tea   ^b *give you*
Tae keep your belly ^cwarm!   ^c pron. *waw-rum*

Besides the songs that may be sung in the back-green, there are many back-green chants:

It's Rainin . . .

✜ It's rainin', it's snawin',
It's cock-a-doodle-doo!

Or sometimes:

✜ It's rainin', it's snawin',
It's cock-a-doodle-dawin'!

These are chanted, usually in March, but sometimes in April, during showers of rain mixed with feathery snowflakes, while the children circle around with their arms held out like birds' wings.

Sticks and Stanes

✜ Sticks and ^astanes'll bre'k ma ^bbanes   ^a *stones*
But names'll never hurt me!   ^b *bones*

✜ "I dinnie [don't] care what ye ca' me, so long as ye dinnie ca' me owre [knock me over]."

Back-green football[8] often has to be confined to heading the

---

[8] The trouble boys get into, playing football in the green or in the street, is at least as old as the ballad *Sir Hugh of Lincoln*:

> He keppit the ba' wi' his foot
> And catcht it with his knee
> And even in at the Jew's window
> He gart the bonny ba' flee.
>
> "Cast oot the ba' to me fair maid
> Cast oot the ba' to me!"
> "Ah, never a bit of it," she says,
> "Till ye come up to me!"

ball, which used to be called "neegerin' ['niggering']," and now is generally called "heiders" or "headering." Other football pastimes are "shootin' in," "crossin'," and "keepie-uppie." And here are several more:

Shapes

✧ This is a game that requires only one goal. The goal is chalked out against a wall. More than two players may take part. Each in his turn must score a goal or be out. The goal may be scored directly or the ball may come off one or more walls or obstacles. The ball must be first-timed and it must hit the goal once and once only. The player of skill devises a "shape" so that the scoring ball comes off at such an angle that the next player finds it difficult or even impossible to score.

Tournaments, or Long Bangin'

✧ "Some'dy goes blindie or bogies [i.e., covers his eyes with the back of his sleeve], and one of the other laddies goes numberer —he numbers a' those that want to play—and the yin [one] that's blindie or bogies says 'Three plays One, Seven plays Four,' or something like that. It's like a kind o' Cup Draw. One goes in one goal and one goes in the other, and they have long bangs [kicks] at each other's goal. Half-time is one goal, three goals wins. In the final, three goals is half-time, and seven goals full-time, and that laddie wins the tournament."

Tippie-tappie

✧ This is played rather like the football in Tournaments. But here, only the inside of the foot is used to hit the ball and the ball must be first-timed [hit once and once only].

Three & You're in

✧ "One is goalie and he throws the ba' oot to the others. They dribble and fight for the ba' and when they get near the goal, they shoot. When some'dy scores three goals he's the new goalie."

Wembley

✧ "The goalie is (say) 'England' and we're 'Scotland.' We're not supposed to go into the penalty box and he's not supposed to come out. The game starts with him flinging the ball out and we must head it in, we mustn't kick it. Scotland must be outside the penalty area. If we kick the ball, it's a goal to the goalie, or if we head it over the bye-line, that's a goal to him tae [too]."

A street football team is often jocularly called the "Back-green Windie-Breckers (window-breakers)."

↭ "We call ourselves the 'Halmyre Street Humdingers,'" and there's the 'Kirkgate Huns'."

Finally, here are some of the other games that can be played in the back-green:

Ala Baba

↭ One of the players stands out, keeping a ball hidden in her clasped hands, while the rest stand in a row with their hands cupped. Passing along the row, the one with the ball recites this rhyme:

> Ala Baba, Ala Baba,
> Who's got the ball?
> I haven't got it
> In my pocket:
> Ala Baba, Ala Baba,
> Who's got the ball?

Meanwhile she discreetly drops the ball into someone else's cupped hands. The player on whom the rhyme ends then guesses who's got the ball. If she guesses right, then it's her turn to stay out: if not, the same player retrieves the ball, and goes on playing the same part as before.

Backies

↭ The old game of two children standing back to back, linking their arms and then lifting each other off their feet, turn about. Long ago the one would cry "Wee [weigh] cheese! and the other "Wee butter!" Or chant: "Wee butter, Wee cheese, Wee a pund, O' candle grease."

Barrie Races

↭ When a boy says "Gies a barrie" he wants his chum to lift his hind legs up like the handles of a barrow so that he can be propelled forward the same as a wheelbarrow.

Best Falls

✧ "Someone has, or pretends to have a gun, and shoots at you all in turn. The one that falls dead the most natural gets the chance of holding and shooting the gun."

Best Man Falls Dead

✧ "This is a game of cowboys and Indians. The cowboy's got the gun. All the Indians take up their positions. They're numbered, and they attack the cowboy in the order of their numbers. When they are all lying dead, the cowboy tickles them under the chin, and the deadest is the next cowboy. The cowboy always wins."

Blind Man's Bluff

✧ A new name for an old game; also called "Ghosties."

Buttonie

✧ Buttons are laid in a row, and the player moistens his thumb and attempts to lift up into his other palm as many buttons as possible. There's another game of the same name in which you chant:

Tinker, tailor, soldier, sailor,
Rich man, poor man, beggarman, thief.

And, while chanting, "ye coont out on the buttons o' your coat and jeans and blouse, or anything, and see who you're going to marry." The same chant also is skipped to.

Cat & Bat

✧ Also called "Cat and Ball," or "Catty," or "Piggy," or "Tippenny." A pointed stick (or a ball) is tipped up into the air, and then the player strikes it with another stick. The aim is to send the first stick (or the ball) as far as possible.

Cat & Mouse

✧ A game for several players: "They a' sit in a circle and ye pick two people and one stands in the middle and one stands at the side where they're sittin'. Someone outside the circle counts 'One, two, three,' up to 'ten,' and shouts 'Go!' And the side one chases the middle one."

C

Champers

✧ A game of "playing at shops." Various coloured stones are "champed [pulverised]" on window-sills of ground-floor houses, and the powders produced are named "tea," "sugar," "coffee," and so forth. The currency used usually consists of "piggy money [broken bits of crockery]," or "glessy money [*i.e.*, bits of coloured glass]."

Chick-a-meltie, or Tick-tack

✧ "Ye tie a button to two bits o' threid [thread], one long and one short. The short bit is stuck to a woman's windie [window] wi' a wee dad [piece] o' chewin' gum. Then ye hide oot o' sight and ye start pu'in' the long threid and it makes a noise."

Click Click

✧ "One person stands out, and he thinks of a word for this game and says it—supposing it's 'pub.' Then the first o' his pals claps his hands three times and says 'whisky,' and the next claps his hands three times and says 'malt,' and the next the same and says 'barley.' And that goes on until somebody gets stuck, and they're out." Some players, before they announce their words, hit their knees with the palms of their hands or hold up both arms and snap their fingers.

Collie-Backie Fights

✧ "Gie's [give us] a collie" is the Scots for "Give me a pick-a-back"; and in the playground "Collie-backie Fights" are very popular with boys. You play in pairs and one boy in each pair is the "horse," while the other "rides" on his back, or is lifted like a bag of coals. Besides "Collie-Backie Fights," there also are "High Shoother [shoulder] Fights," or "High Shooder Fights," in which each of the fighters sits on another boy's shoulders instead of clinging to his back.

Conkers

✧ No sport brings a greater zest to the approach of autumn. Horse chestnuts become conker trees then, and in search of them the laddies sally far and wide.

In preparation for the game, a hole is bored in the chestnut or conker which is then threaded on to a stout piece of twine or a boot-lace. This has to be knotted near the end in order to hold the conker. A string loaded with spare conkers usually accompanies each player.

Contestants try, shot about, to destroy each other's conker. A fresh conker overwhelming an opponent, also a beginner, becomes a bully-one (or one-er). If it smashes another beginner, it becomes a bully-two (or two-er). But battle honours are added on so that a bully-two which shatters a bully-seven becomes a bully-nine. "Last year I had a bully-hunder."

"Tangles" (i.e. a second shot) is claimed when your opponent's conker by not being held properly, gives rise to a mishit. A "cheesie" is an oval chestnut with a flat top. The hardening of conkers gets the name of being a very subtle art:

"I steep mine in vinegar and then leave them in the oven for a whole night."

"I keep them for a year."

"I bury the conkers in the groond for a day or two."

Cuddie Hunkers[9]

✧ "Ye pick two evenly matched sides, and one o' the sides a' line up one after the other wi' their heids tucked down. The first one leans against a wall, or on a boy who stands against the wa'. Then the others a' come up and one by one jump on to the leaning backs; and when they're a' on, they try to make these 'cuddies [donkeys]' collapse. The cuddies win if they can manage to keep them a' up for a count of ten; if they dinnie [don't], they're cuddies a' owre [over] again." Also called "Cuddie Wechts [weights]" or "Cuddie-Gie [give]-Wey [way]" or "Cuddie Lowps [jumps]."

Do This, Do That

✧ The players imitate the actions of person speaking, but only when the command is "Do this!" A move at "Do that!" puts the player "out the game."

Donkey

✧ A ball-game for several players. The players make a ring, and the one with the ball stands in the middle and throws it to any of the other players. The first time any player drops it, that player is *D*, the next time *D-O*, and so on. As soon as any player is *D-O-N-K-E-Y*, that player is "out," and leaves the ring; and the last who is left stands in the middle for the next game.

[9] "Hunkers" is the Scots, Scotch or Scoatch for "haunches."

Dotto

⋄ Also called "Ditto": the same as "Statues," or "Stookies."

French Cricket

⋄ Game played with a round stick as bat and any kind of small ball—usually a "golfie [golf ball]." The ball is aimed at the batter's legs, which serve as wickets. The batsman must not shift the position he first takes up—otherwise he's out. He can be bowled at, and out, from any angle. He scores by hitting the ball away from him and counts one run by passing the batting stick once round his back. A rule is laid down that he musn't hit the ball further away than say, twelve jumps. If there is any doubt that he has done so, he may be asked by the bowler to "step it"—that is, see whether he ran reach the dead ball within twelve jumps. If he can't, he's out.

Another game on similar lines using the batsman's legs as wickets is called "Missie-blockie." It's played with the ordinary cricket bat and ball and the bowling is likewise from near at hand and of a gentle sort.

Hal-a-leevoy

⋄ One of the oldest games is A-leevoy (or Leevoy, or Relieve-oy, or Relieve-o or Relievers,) which has been played for hundreds of years. Barley Break,[10] much the same sort of game, is now quite unknown. In A-leevoy you have a den and one of the players is het. The one that's het has to catch all the others and each one he catches is put in the den. But all the prisoners may be instantly set free by any player still at large. His task is to run up stealthily and thrust a foot across the line of the den. At this moment of triumph he always cries out: "A-leevoy!"

Nowadays instead of one person being het and having to capture all the others, there's a growing popularity for playing the game as between two teams. The one team runs away and

[10] Alexander Scott (*c.* 1530-*c.* 1584), "Of May":
    In May goes *ᵃ*dammosalis and dammis   *ᵃgirls and women*
    In gardens green to play like lambs;
    Some at the bairis they brace like billeis
    Some rins at "Barlabreikis" like rams,
    Some round about the standard *ᵇ*pilleis.   *ᵇpillars*

the other team has to catch them. "We play 'lassies *versus* laddies.'" "We play it a lot in the street and our rules are ye've to keep to the block, jist the pavements or the back-greens and that,—but no across the road."

In England our game of A-leevoy is called Prisoners' Base and in France it's called *Jeu de Barres*. In both countries the game is begun by first picking sides. Readers of Proust may recollect that Marcel himself used to play A-leevoy in the Champs-Elysées and that one day when he turned up late, his girl friend Gilberte greeted him rather sharply with a: "Hurry up for a game of Leevoy—you're on my side!"

Before the 1920s the game in Edinburgh was generally called Leevoy or A-leevoy. Since then the name has gradually changed to Hal-a-leevoy or Hallie-leevoy. Although at first hearing, this would appear to be a newer name, in point of fact it's older. The name long ago was Hell and today the middle part of the English den still gets the name of hell. Hell here means not only the infernal regions but refers also to a goddess of ancient Norway who was a kind of Proserpine.

Half-past

- The one that's "het ['it']" goes along the row of players asking "Half-past . . .?" The idea is to guess the hour that's being thought of—like "half-past nine." To relieve the tedium, there are some stock funny answers, such as "Half-past my Grannie's shirt tail," or "Half-past a man going doun the stairs wi' a bag o' coal on his back."

Halt

- An outdoor game. "Someone takes the ball and throws it up in the air and shout's someone's name, and they go and get the ball, and the other children run away, and the girl or boy with the ball shouts: 'Halt!' and everybody stops, and the person with the ball guesses and takes so many steps to reach each person and touch them with the ball, and they are out. If she guesses wrong she has to start again to guess right from wherever she is. The last touched is out for the next game."

Hoppy Diggy

- In Hoppy Diggy, usually played between two sides, you have to hop on one leg and try to dig your hopping opponent off both.

Houses

❖ Pronounced "hoossis." An ever-popular game of make-belief in which the characters are Father, Mother, and the Children, and the rooms of the house are outlined in chalk or by stones.

Horses

❖ Playing at horses is an old and cherished pastime, and most often to the singing of:

> Hey, gee up ma cuddie
> Ma cuddie's owre the dyke:
> And if ye touch ma cuddie
> Ma cuddie'll gie ye a bite!

In the Lothians the word "cuddie" can mean a horse as well as a donkey.

I Love Coffee

❖ A ring-game played with a ball, chanting:

> I love coffee
> I love tea
> How many ªfellies   ª *fellows*
> Are sweet on me?

I Want

❖ "You sit in a circle or row (maybe in an entry for the rain) and the first person says, 'I want a car'; and the second says, 'I want a car and a bike'; and the third says, 'I want a car and a bike and a pram'; and the first one to forget anything or make a mistake is out the game, and the one who's best at remembering is the winner."

King o' the Castle

❖ The idea is to keep command of a high place, usually a wall, chanting:

> I'm the King o' the Castle
> And you're the dirty wee rascal!

"The King," as it is more often called, is still popular.

Keppers

❖ A simple game, in which two or more "keppers [catchers]" throw a ball (or indeed anything throwable) to each other in turn, and, by counting, find out how long they can keep it up.

King Ball

❖ A game played with a "fullie [(rhymes with sully) full-sized football]." When the ball is thrown at you, you have to catch it between your clenched fists.

A Lammie

❖ A trick played on someone who has too readily believed your story or account of some matter—and which is, of course, untrue.

Last Touch

❖ "Last Touch," or "Last Nip," or "Last Whistle," is played by children when taking leave of one another. "First Nip," on the other hand, is administered to anyone wearing anything *new* for the first time. Another game involving a nip is "Pass it on!"

Mary Queen of Scots

❖ You chant these words:

> Mary Queen of Scots
> Got her head chopped off—
> Just like this!

—"And ye wheech [whip] the head off a yellow dandelion or dandelion clock."

❖ There is another game in which you chant:

> Mary Queen of Scots
> Got her head chopped off
> Her head chopped off
> Mary Queen of Scots
> Got her head chopped off
> Her head chopped off—
> Like this!"

"You play with a ball in a stocking which is banged against a wall and through your legs."

❖ Yet another version (a great favourite in the school playground) runs:

> Mary, Queen of Scots
> Got her head chopped off
> Got her head chopped off
> Got her head chopped off
> Mary, Queen of Scots
> Got her head chopped off
> O F F!

"Ye get a lassie and you hud [hold] one of her feet at the back. Then somebody takes her right airm and another her left airm and ye bounce her up and doun in the air as ye say the words. At *O F F* she goes up right high."

Missie Kickie

❖ A game that is played by girls as well as boys. The players form a square and the ball is kicked from one player to any other player. If you twice touch it, or twice miss it, you're out the game.

My Father is . . .

❖ "Ye pick someone to be out and they say 'My father is . . .' and they do the action, such as window-cleaning, or engine-driving, or cobbling; and the folk who watch guess and the person who guesses right is out next."

Odd Man Out

❖ A gambling game based on spinning pennies. In the same category are "Odds and Evens," "Heading," and "Head Man Guesses." In "Pitch and Toss" the coins are thrown.

"One, Two, Three—Show!"

❖ In this game your two first fingers held up, V-shaped means: "Scissors!"; your hand cupped with fingers sticking up: "Fire!"; your hand the same way only upside down with fingers drooping: "Rain!" or "Water!"; your clenched fist: "Stane [stone]!" or "Rock!"; your hand flat, palm downwards, and pointing outwards: "Paper!"

Two boys, opposite each other, with their right hands behind their backs, begin with a "One, two three—*show!*" and then simultaneously shape their clenched fists before them into any one of the configurations, laid down. Well, between the two, who wins?

"The laddie that gets the better one wins."

The better one is decided by accepted ideas like: stone wins over fire, because stone can put out fire; water wins over stone because water wears stone away: fire wins over paper because fire can burn paper; paper wins over stone because paper can wrap round stone. Or stone blunts scissors, scissors cut paper, rain rusts scissors while fire melts them—the full list is somewhat long.

"Ye dinnie really think what things ye're gaun to make. That's the fun o' it."

"But the yin that wins wets his first two fingers and he's allowed to slap the back o' the loser's wrist. And ye keep on playing until one boy's wrist is that sair, he disnie want tae play any mair."

"When ye baith dae the same things ye just start owre again."

Open the Doors

⋄ "Open the doors" is sometimes shouted by boys as a jeering rhyme:

> Open the doors!
> Shut the doors!
> Shake the doors!
> Diana Dors!

It can also be used by girls for a "Single Ballie," the player straddling her legs, then bringing them together, then wiggling herself and finally "acting Diana Dors."

Pass the Parcel

⋄ More a party game. In the street or back-green a tune is hummed or played on a mouth organ, and you're out if you're caught with the parcel when the tune stops.

Running Races

⋄ Races among the bairns are nearly always started with the rhyme:

> One to be ready:
> Two to be steady:
> Three to be off!

"In oor back-green we aye make the rhyme:

> Three to be perfect
> And four to be off!"

Scraps

⊸ Highly-coloured, rather old-fashioned and punched-out pictures, sold in sheets by stationers. The scrap-playing age ranges from five to eleven. Boys sometimes take up this game, but only among themselves, and only with scraps featuring cars, aeroplanes, trains, ships, or rockets; and girls are much more faithful followers of it.

The treasured scraps are kept between the leaves of some old book—the bigger, the better. Early and middle summer is the season for playing. The girls go about with the scrap-books under their "oxters [armpits]"; then they sit down in the sun and begin to "swop [exchange]."

Before swopping, two girls usually start by exchanging scrap-books. Each then pulls out the ones she would like, leaving them sticking out like book-marks. A little later each gets back her own book, and now they see whether they can agree to part with the scraps selected.

The scraps to be exchanged may differ in size or in status. Angels (and "holy ones" or "holies") have the highest status, and after that the scale runs: Brides, Flowery Girls and Flowery Boys, Roses, Baskets of Flowers, Babes, Figures ("like wi' crinolines"), Nationalities, Animals, Clowns, Birds, Royalty ("pit them at the end"). For scraps of equal quality the swopping is done on an area basis.

In Edwardian days the soldier scrap was always referred to as "Pontius Pilate." Nowadays girls prefer scraps that were made "before the War."—"Pre-war-ies". These are much duller in colour, but here (as elsewhere) rarity counts. Even a home-made scrap (cut from a coloured magazine) might achieve a high local value.

Semolina

⊸ "This is a gemm o' hidin' seek where naebody goes to look for anybody. Ye play it in an entry [stairway]. The yin that's het hides his face for a wee while and the yins that are hidin' cry oot 'Come oan!' And he turns roond and says: 'Alec's in Broon's!' or 'Alec's in Green's!' or 'Alec's in the back passage!' If he's wrong, naebody'll come oot, if he's right that person's now het. Broon's means roond in the coarner [corner] in Broon's doorway, Green's in Green's doorway and if he had cried 'Alec's in Broon's' when Alec was really hidin' in Green's, then Alec can safely come oot then for he cannie be het."

Seven Stanie

❖ "Ye collect aboot seven tin cans and stack them on tope o' each other against a wa'. Then ye pick two sides. It's really a chasing game but it's kind o' complicated. Ye toss up to see which side gets chased. This side gets to throw the ba' at thae cans from a medium distance. The other side splits up into two and each half fields on either side o' the cans. If the thrower misses the cans and the ba' is co't efter bouncin' off the wa' and stottin' once, then he's oot the game. He's as good as co't. If he has three shots and misses the cans and disnie get co't, he gets a 'life,' that means he can start a' owre again. But if he's oot, somebody else o' his side has to come and take a chance o' throwin' the ba'. If the cans are hit doun (they have tae fa'), everybody on that side scarpers, and the fielding side has to chase efter them. Tae catch them they're jist to be hit wi' the ba'. Usually the chasing side bunch thegither to begin wi' so that the other side dinnie ken which o' them's gote the ba' hidden doun his juke [jumper]. If somebody manages to slip past the chasers, and gets back to the cans and sets them up again, then his side gets their shoats at the cans a' owre again. Ye aye have a laddie guardin' the cans to stope this happenin'— he gets the ba' thrown to him when there's any danger o' this.

Some folk ca' the gemm Seven Cannie."

Silence in Court

❖ Somebody recites the words:

> Silence in the Court—
> The Monkey wants to speak:
> Speak, Monkey, speak!

And the first person who breaks the ensuing silence is the Monkey.

Silhouettes

❖ Making animals' shadows on a sunny wall using your hands and fingers. Favourite silhouettes: Butterfly, Duck, Dog, Eagle, Ostrich, Rabbit, Reindeer, Rook, Swan, Wolf.

Snowman

⟣ Someone stands out, eyes shut, and raised arms kept waving up and down. You've to run underneath these arms without being touched. If you are, then you've to take a turn of being "Snowman."

Steps

⟣ "Ye stand at the top o' a stair, and the idea is to reach the stair-foot. If you've got anything red on, say, ye're tellt ye can go down one step or two. And so on for colours. But when you reach the ground level, as soon as you put one foot down, the one that's out and has been giving the directions has to catch hold of you before you can scramble back to the top of the stair again."

Stookies[11]

⟣ "One person is out. He or she shuts their eyes and turns their back to the others, who do a dance, or pretend they're cleaning windows or ice-skating. When the person opens their eyes and turns round, everybody must stop in whatever position they happen to be in." The next person out is either the best "stookie," or the one who keeps motionless longest. To break down the resistance of the "stookies," the person that's out can tickle them under the chin. "That's the game we cry [call] 'Best Man Falls Dead'."

The older game of Stookies used to be started by the one that was out taking all the others in turn and "birling" them round and round—and then they "went stookie [turned into stucco]."

There is yet another game of Stookies, in which "a girl lies flat on a dyke and another is chosen to press the buttons on her cardigan, starting from the top one. The top button, when pressed, raises an arm; the second button jerks out the other arm; the third and fourth buttons, the legs. After pressing the last button, the girl who was lying on the dyke gets up and walks about stookie, and so do all the rest of the players."

"To walk about stookie" is to go about like an automaton conceived after the fashion set by *Frankenstein* and culminating in the "robot" depicted by Karel Čapek in his play *R.U.R.* This idea, among children, matured long before the appearance on television of the Daleks.

---

[11] Stucco (plaster of Paris) statues.

Sugar Baby

❖ "You stand in a row, and one person stands out and birls everybody round and lets them go; and wherever you land, you lie down on your stomach and hide your eyes, and anybody that moves has to get up, and everybody gets up then; and the last person up, before she gets up, everybody goes round her and shouts 'Sugar Baby!' "

Sunday, Monday

❖ Seven players take the names of the days of the week. An eighth (who's "het") throws the ball high against a wall and shouts some day of the week, say Friday. "Friday" has first to catch the ball and then hit one of the seven, who have now taken to their heels. The one hit is "het" for the next game.

Tap-a-Door-Run-fast

❖ As can be imagined, a game for the mischievous. Also called "Ring, Bang, Scoosh," which is explained in this way: " 'Ring! —ye ring the bell; 'Bang!'—ye kick the door; 'Scoosh!'—ye run for it."

Tattie Bogle[12]

❖ A potato made into a frightening figure by sticking burnt-out matches into it.

The Red Queen Frowns

❖ A ring-game, in which one player (the Red Queen) goes in the middle, and the rest chant:

> The Red Queen frowns
> The Red Queen stamps:
> Madam, what do you want?

"Then the Red Queen chooses something she would like the rest to act, and as they act it, she picks the best one, and that one becomes the Red Queen."

There was a Wee Man

❖ There was a wee man
Who lived in a pan

---

[12] A "bogle" means a spectre or apparition.

The pan was too wee
So he lived in the sea
The sea was too wide
So he lived in the tide
And a' the wee fishes
Ran up his backside!

"Ye jine [join] hands and go round in a circle, a' the lassies wi'
their backs to another lassie who stands in the middle. And she
says the rhyme and as she says it, she taps ye on the back at
each word, and when she comes to backside she kicks ye and
that yin [one] goes into the middle and ye do it again.

Naebody else kens that game. Only the people in oor street—
Loganlea Road!"

They're Going to Build a House

◇ A chorus game:

They're going to build a house—
BOO!—a public house—*HURRAY!*
They're only going to have one bar—
BOO!—a mile long—*HURRAY!*
They're not going to serve the beer in glasses—
BOO!—but in buckets—*HURRAY!*
They're only going to have one barmaid—
BOO!—for each customer—*HURRAY!*
They're going to dilute the beer—
BOO!—with whisky—*HURRAY!*
They're going to close at ten—
BOO!—in the morning—*HURRAY!*

Tin Rugby

◇ "You get two bins or buckets and ye get a large ball. Ye have
an equal number of players on each side. Ye place the buckets
at a fair distance from each other and right opposite each other.
Each side tries to get the ball inside the other side's bucket.
The ball can be passed by kicking or throwing backwards or
forwards, but if you're touched when you've got the ball, you
must leave it or drop it at once."

Tipenny-Nipenny

◇ Leapfrog, played by players bending down and jumping over
in strict alternation, was a favourite game in the 1900s.

Truth, Dare, Double Dare, Promise, or Repeat

One boy or girl stands out. The rest sit in a circle. The 'outer' picks on one of them and says 'Truth, Dare, Double Dare, Promise, or Repeat.'

If they choose 'Truth,' you could ask: 'Who were you at the pictures with last night?' And they have to tell the truth.

For 'Dare,' you ask the person to chap on Grannie Somebody's door and then run away.

For 'Double Dare,' they could be asked to kiss somebody.

For 'Promise,' you could be made to say 'I love So-and-So' a hundred times.

For 'Repeat' ye make them say efter you something horrible or daft or no true—one word at a time."

Instead of 'Repeat,' some say 'Command'; and sometimes an empty bottle is sent spinning round and round on the ground and whoever it points to has to do the 'Dare.' In this game it has to be an awfie [awfully] hard 'Dare'—a 'Devil Dare'."

"In oor street we say 'Truth, Dare, Double Dare, Promise or Repeat, Kiss or Cuddle. If ye say 'Kiss' ye get tellt maybe to kiss that lamp-post twenty times. Or the groond! And for 'Cuddle' ye've maybe to cuddle a lamp-post. Ye look a right nut."

Tuffet Fights

Fights between different back-greens or different streets using tufts, tuffies, tuffets or divots of grass. In "gress fights ye yase [use] the wee short-cut gress, row'd [rolled] into ba's."

2

CHOOSING SIDES AND COUNTING-OUT RHYMES

For most games quite a number of players are needed, and very often "calling-rhymes" are sung or chanted in the stairways or up to the kitchen windows of playmates to make them hurry up (or down).

Weary Weary

◇ Weary, weary, waiting on you,
I can wait no longer on you,
Three times I've whistled on you:
Are you coming out?

Tommy Simpson

◇ Hi, Tommy Simpson, are ye no' comin' oot
[a]Tae see a' the monkeys jumpin' aboot   [a] to
Wi' their hands in their [b]pooches   [b] pockets
And their tails [c]hingin' oot?   [c] hanging
Aw, Tommy Simpson, are ye no comin' oot?

Once the players have been assembled and the game chosen, the next job is to find out who is to be "het," who is to be "out," or who is to be the "outer." A "Counting-out Rhyme" often decides. Some of these rhymes in current use have served this purpose for centuries.

According to Dr John Brown (author of *Rab and His Friends*), Pet Marjorie (in 1810) put Walter Scott through his paces in two counting-out rhymes which he pretended he had half-forgotten:

◇ Ziccotty dicotty dock
The mouse ran up the clock
The clock struck wan
Down the mouse ran
Ziccotty dicotty dock.

❖ Wunnery tooery tickery seven
Alibi crackaby ten and eleven
Pin pan musky dan
Tweedle-um twoddle-um twenty-wan
Eerie orie ourie—
You are out!

Many similar rhymes belonging to the "Eentie teentie" pattern continue to circulate:

❖ Eentie teentie tithery mithery bamfileerie
Hover dover—you are out!

❖ Eentie teentie terry erry ram tam toosh,
Go to the cellar, catch a wee [a]mouse: [a] pron. *mooss*
Cut it up in slices, fry it in the pan,
Mind and leave the gravy for the wee fat man!

The younger children tend to use the simpler rhymes:

❖ One, two
Sky blue
All out
But you!

❖ Easie, osie,
Man's [a]brosie,   [a] *brose*
Easie, osie,
Out!

But they probably choose this one most:

My Mother & Your Mother

❖ "My mother and your mother
Were hanging out their clothes
My mother gave your mother
A [a]dunt on the nose: [a] *punch*
What was the colour of the blood?"
"Green."
"G R E E N spells 'green'—
You are out!"

D

Some of the rhymes like "Queen Queen Caroline" or "Six White Horses in a Stable" go in a direct fashion to the person the rhyme ends on—who is therefore *out*.

✧ Queen Queen Caroline
Dipped her hair in turpentine
Turpentine made it shine
Queen Queen Caroline.

✧ Six white horses in a stable
Pull one out and call it Mabel
Mabel Mabel set the table
Six white horses in a stable.

Other rhymes make the occasion into a little drama by demanding a choice of name or number or the spelling of a word or number; and this also allows the players room for manoeuvre so that the last word will not be falling on them:

A Party on the Hill

✧ "There's a party on the hill:
Will you come?
Bring your own cup and saucer and a bun:
Who is your loved one?"

"John."

"John will be there
Kissing Jeanie in the chair—
There's a party on the hill:
Will you come?"

A Bottle of Ink

✧ "A bottle of ink
Fell down the sink
How many inches did it run?"

"Three."

"*T H R E E* spells 'three'—
You are out!"

My Wee Jeanie

❖ "My wee Jeanie
  Has a nice clean ᵃpeenie   ᵃ *pinafore*
  And guess what colour it was?'

"Red."

"*R E D* spells that bonny bonny colour of red, and if you
have it on, you go out of this game with a slap on the face!"

"Is there another version of this rhyme that ends differently?"

"Oh yes!"

"Let's hear it."

"*R E D* spells that bonny bonny colour of red, and if
you have it on, you go out of this game with a slap on the
jaw!"

One Potato Two Potato

❖ Very popular rhyme with boys and girls. Also called Tatties.
The players hold out their clenched fists—potatoes—and the
one who counts out the rhyme also has her fists clenched. As
she strikes each fist in turn with her fist she keeps chanting the
couplet:

> One potato, two potato, three potato, four:
> Five potato, six potato, seven potato, more!

On whatever fist the word "more" falls, that fist gets tucked
behind the player's back, and if, as the rhyme progresses, the
Counter-Out happens to get two of *her* fists tucked behind her
back, she then counts with nods of her head. Normally she
counts her potatoes against her mouth. Whoever's left with
one or two "potatoes" held out is "het" for the game that's to
be played.

Spin the Bottle

❖ Another game which is a game in its own right but mostly is
used for settling who's to be "het." The bottle is placed long-
ways on the ground and spun round until it stops—pointing at
someone.

Tickam-Tackam

✧ Also called "Tickie-Tackie." To pick sides, two leaders measure the distance between them in single footsteps, and the last to get a complete foot in the diminishing space, wins. As each places a foot, the words "Tickam" and "Tackam" are said alternately and accordingly.

This method of choosing goes back at least a hundred years. Nowadays it's called chiefly "Tick and Tack," and the object of the two contestants is now slightly different. The winner of this walking-bout is the first to tread on his opponent's toe. When "Tick and Tack" is in prospect, one or other shouts out: "Everything for me and nowts for you." This right enables him to take the avoiding action of "Heelie" or "Toeie" and the obstructing action of "Kneeie," or he can go "Round the World" that is, place his foot at different angles making a roundabout journey. "Tick and Tack" can also be played "Plain."

Blind Man

✧ Also called "Bogie." Another game for picking sides. "If ye want to pick sides, one o' the laddies goes and hides his face, and one person gies everybody a number and the 'Blind Man' shouts the number, one for one side, one for the other."

To pick out the girl who's to stand in the middle in a Ring-Game, one player shuts her eyes, the rest take numbers, and this player chooses a number, or she says a colour, and the one wearing that colour goes in the middle.

Twenty-one Picks a Pal

✧ "A game in which ye coont [count] everybody in a row and whaever is 21, he picks another laddie. Then ye go roond again for 21, and he picks his pal—until ye've got your two sides."

Burnt Matches

✧ "Ye brek bits off matchsticks, and, hidin' them between your hands like that, only showin' the burnt heids [heads], whoever picks the wee-est is 'het.' Ye can dae the same wi' straws or blades o' gress. Whaeever pulls oot the biggest gets "first pick" or "shoot up" or "shoot doun"—if ye're playing at fitba'."

Wet or Dry

✧ A game to see who's to get first pick. "One player runs his two palms (one after the other) down over his face, and past his tongue, and then he holds them before him, backs upward, and asks someone to choose "Wet "or "Dry."

Last to the Den's Het

❖ A game in which everybody runs to the den, and that decides it. "Sometimes, to see who's het, a round den is outlined with six wee chalked crosses—made by the Dennie (that's a 'Black Sheep' or a wee laddie, or one that's been counted out in 'Twenty-One') and someone shouts, 'Hot Peas and Vinegar!' and ye all race to that Den."

Hands in the Tub

❖ Or "in the Basket." Another useful game. "If there's a difference o' opinion on what game to play, one o' the laddies clasps his hands and huds his airms like an arc in front o' him, and he cries 'Hands in the tub a' them that want to play at Kick-the-Can!' and a' them that agree dips their right or left airm 'in the tub.' Or it might be, 'Hands in the basket who want to play Hidie-Go!' and it's the same sort o' thing."

The Whispering Way

❖ "Every yin in turn whispers the gemm he'd maist like to play to this one person, and that person tells ye efter what gemm has won."

Heads or Tails

❖ Tossing a coin and crying "Heads" or "Tails" is another method of picking sides which is more favoured by boys than by girls. When the decision of chance goes against you, to undo it, you shout "Best o' three," which means tossing the coin once or twice again, so that the original decision is either confirmed or reversed. When the tossed coin lands on the ground, if it's "Heads," the boy who has foretold this usually tries to get in a quick cry of "Heads-nae best o' three!" so that the loser is out-manoeuvred.

Sherp or Blunt

❖ Another method of picking sides is to hold a pencil flat between the palms of your hand and ask, "Sherp or Blunt?"

A Cock or a Hen

If two sides are already playing and someone comes along and pleads, "Gie's a gemm [game]," as often as not he's told to wait for "A Cock or a Hen"—In other words, until another boy turns up, then each can name himself "Cock" or "Hen," and the leaders of the sides can then choose one or the other, probably after a preliminary wrangle about who is to get "First Cry" or: "It's me—you got the cry the last time."

Instead of "A Cock or a Hen, the two boys might choose between: "A Car or a Lorry"; "A Pin or a Needle"; "A Bap or a Scone"; "A Truck or an Engine"; "A Cat or a Mouse"; "An Apple or an Orange"; "A Ship or a Cruiser"; "A Can or a Bottle"; "A Diesel or a Steamie"; "A Liner or a Trawler"; "A Rocket or a Plane."

"Barley,"[1] or "Barleys," or "Barley Bees," or "Bees" (thumbs up), all are cries or signs for a truce in any game.

Here is a selection of "counting-out rhymes," old and new:

⤷   A B C
My Grannie caught a flea
She salted it and peppered it
And took it for her tea.

There are numerous variants. Often the rhyme begins "One two three" or "Dearie, dearie, me." But the flea catcher is invariably "my grannie" or "my mother," and in her generation grannie "catched" her flea.

⤷   Apples peaches pears and plums
When does your birthday come?

You then count out the number of days in the birthday (if, for example, it's on the seventh of the month in which it falls, the number is seven), and the one it finishes on is out.

⤷   A wee wee [a]teuchie-bird   [a] *peeweep, peewit;*
Lol lol lol   i.e., *lapwing*
Laid an egg on the [b]windie-sole: [b] *window-sill*
When the windie-sole began to crack
The wee wee teuchie-bird roared and [c]grat.   [c] *wept*

⤷   As I was walking down Inky Pinkie Lane
I met some Inky Pinkie soldiers
I asked them what colour their flag was
And they said: "Red, white and blue."

---

[1] Variously explained as coming from "by our Lady" or "parley."

✧ As I went up the apple tree
All the apples fell on me:
Make a pudding, bake a pie,
Send it up to Lord Mackay.

Lord Mackay's no in,
Send it to the Man in the ᵃMune   ᵃ *moon*
The Man in the Mune's mendin' ᵇshoon,   ᵇ *shoes*
Tuppence the pair and they're a' ᶜdune.   ᶜ *done*

✧ Boy Scout
Walk out
Girl Guide
Step aside.

Counting out with this rhyme has links with One Potato,
two potato. But instead of fists, feet are dealt with. Each player
points her right foot into a common centre—forming a sort of
star. The Counter-Out then repeats the rhyme indicating with
her finger each foot in the passing. At the word "aside" that
player withdraws her right foot and replaces with her left.
If the "aside" falls on her again, she withdraws entirely, and
the person left in last is het.

✧ Eat me, teat me, terry berry, ram tam toosh
ᵃGaun ablow the bed and find a wee fat ᵇmoose ᵃ *go in under*
Cut him up in slices, fry him in a pan   ᵇ *mouse*
Mind and keep the gravy for the wee fat man!

✧ Eenie meenie maka raka ay eye
Ay eye domma
Chika poka pam pam push.

✧ Eenie meenie maka raka
Ray rye domin aka
Cheeka poka la la poka
Am pam push.

✧ Eenie meenie mina mo
Catch a nigger by the toe
When he squeals let him go
Eenie meenie mina mo.

✧ Eenie meenie mannie mo
Sit the baby on the po
When he's done, wipe his bum
Eenie meenie mannie mo.

Recently (1963) three "Coronation Street" characters, Ena Sharples, Minnie Caldwell and Martha Longhurst, have gained entry into this age-old rhyme:

⋄   Ena, Minnie, Martha, mo
    To the Rover's they will go
    Drinking stout with all their might
    Ena, Minnie, Martha, mo.

⋄   Eelie olie
    ᵃDug's tolie   *ᵃ dog's excrement*
    Eelie olie
    Out!

⋄   Eentie teentie heathery beathery
    Bam faloram am dan musky dan
    You are out.

⋄   Eentie teentie tuppenny bun
    The cat went out to get some fun
    Got some fun and played the drum
    Eentie teentie tuppenny bun.

⋄   Eerie oarie ickerie am
    Put the vinegar in the pan
    Eerum squeerum boxie leerum
    Cherricks up the castle
    Doun the close
    There stands a bonny white horse
    It can gallop, it can trot
    It can tell who's at home
    Father, mother, dirty Tom.

⋄   Eetle ottle black bottle
    Eetle ottle out!
    Shining on the mantelpiece
    Like a silver threepenny-piece:
    Eetle ottle black bottle
    Eetle ottle out!

⋄   Eetle ottle black bottle
    Eetle ottle out!
    Tea and sugar is my delight
    And *O U T* spells "out"!

✧ Eetle ottle black bottle
  Eetle ottle out,
  If ye want a piece on jam
  Please step out.

✧ Engine, engine, number nine
  Run along the bogey line
  [a]Out, scoot, you're [a]out   [a] pron. *oot*
  Engine, engine, number nine.

Instead of "Oot, scoot" you often hear "Peas scoot"

✧ Hickity pickity, rovie dovie,
  Dinkty tell, ram tam, toosh:
  You are out.

✧ I think, I think
  I smell a stink
  Coming from *Y O U*.

A very intelligent use of spondees!

✧ Inky pinkie hala balum
  The cat went oot to get some fun
  It got a bun
  And away it run
  Inky pinkie hala balum

✧ Queenie, Queenie Caroline-a
  Dipped her hair in turpentine-a
  Turpentine-a made it shine-a
  Queenie, Queenie Caroline-a.

✧ Little Miss Pink
  Fell down the sink
  How many miles do you think she went?
  "Four."
  F O U R, out.

✧ Mickey Mouse
  He bought a house
  What colour do you think it was?
  "Red"
  R E D and out you must go
  For telling me so.

✧ Ra ra joober-a, roenee, ponee, ping-a-ring-a-ra
It-a bit-a west-a canti pooh
It-a bit-a it-a chit-a Chinese Jew.
Eerie orie you are out.

✧ Sister, sister, I've been thinking
What on earth have you been drinking?
Looks like water
Smells like wine
O my gosh it's turpentine!

✧ Three wee ᵃtotties in a pot   ᵃ potatoes
Go and see if one is hot:
If it is, cut its throat
Three wee totties in a pot.

✧ Three white horses in one stable
Pick one out and call it Mabel:
If it's Mabel, set the table
Three white horses in one stable.

✧ Twenty horses in a stable
One jumped in and *O U T*.

✧ Tinker tailor soldier sailor
Rich man poor man beggarman thief.

"The one the word 'thief' falls on can choose any of the names
mentioned to be spelt out—to find who's to be out."

✧ Up the pole
Down the pole
Out goes
Sausage roll.

The Counter-Out points her finger skywards, for the first line,
down to the ground for the second line, and for the rest she
starts counting out in the usual way. It's as though the earth
and the sky were included as players.

✧ "Who's there?"
"Tiny Tiny Bear."
"What do you want?"
"A pint of beer."
"Where's your money?"
"In my pocket."

"Where's your pocket?"
"I forgot it—
And *O U T* spells out."

Although this rigmarole is a dialogue it is spoken entirely by the Counter-out.

⟡ Your shoe is dirty
Your shoe is dirty
So please take it out!

'Say five lassies want to play at Hidie-go, they a' put oot a foot and yin o' them says the rhyme until only one shoe is left in. That lassie's het."

The rhymes of Scotland have emigrated all over the world and what might be their descendants occasionally voyage back to the Old Country. Here, from Adelaide, are a few counting-out rhymes that bring to Auld Reekie the bright sense and colour of the Antipodes:

⟡ A little green snake
Ate too much cake
And now he has
The belly-ache.

⟡ Captain Cook chased a ^a^chook   ^a^ *chicken*
All around Australia
He jumped a fence
And tore his pants
And then he was a sailor.

⟡ Eeny, meeny, myny, mo
Catch a wombat by the toe
If it hollers
Let it go
Eeny, meeny, myny, mo.

⟡ The kookaburra sits on the old gum tree
Merry merry king of the bush is he
Catch the laughing kookaburra
Or you'll go out for three:
T H R E E.

"In Australia the game you cry 'British Bulldog,' we call it 'Red Rover'."

3

CHASIE, TIG, AND HIDE-AND-SEEK

"Chasie," "Tig," and "Hide-and-Seek," must be among the oldest games.

CHASIE

In "Chasie" you have two equal sides, each of any number. One side runs away and the other side have to chase after and catch every one of them. There is no den. The game is played at the earliest age, from five (say) to fourteen—only, the side that gets the chance of running away, the older the players are, the further afield they may be expected to go. "Arrows" is another chasing-game where the seekers are guided by arrows chalked on flagstones, copestones, and walls.

TIG

"Tig—you're het!" is one of the first playing phrases learned by a Scottish child; and another is the rule "Nae tiggin' the butcher," which means you can't tig back the person who has tigged you. In tig, as in any other game, you cry "Barley!" if you want a truce for some purpose—such as tying your shoe-lace. The term "High jinks," which meant that you were exempt from being tigged, was very common up to the 1920s, but nowadays it is little used.

"With how many games of tig," wrote Robert Louis Stevenson, "is Colinton Manse connected in my mind!" We can only guess what kind of tig he played; possibly "Plain Tig." Since his day many new games of tig have been invented. There are well over a dozen forms of it, all very well known:

Aeroplane Tig

↭ "The person that's het has to chase the other ones, and when they're tug, they've to stand still with their arms thrust out like airyplanes. If one of the free ones tigs this one, he can be freed. The first person to be tigged three times is het in the next game."

Blindie Tig

✧ Played on the merry-go-round. "Somebody gets lyin' doun on the groond in the centre o' the merrie. That's the yin that's het, and he has to shut his lamps [eyes]. Aboot four folk lie owre [over] the top o' the merrie and ye spin it roond, and the yin that's het sticks his hand up, and tries to tig somebody. The rest try to get oot his road by rollin' aboot."

Chainie Tig

✧ "If you're het, the first person you tig has to join hands, and you go tigging together, and the next tug joins on, and the next, and the next, until there's no more left, and that first person is het for the next game."

Gatie Tig

✧ "If there's six of you and ye play, there's only five gates, because the one that's het cannie get a gate, and ye've got to change gates, and if the person that's het gets on tae a gate, one of the other people must be het."

High Tig & Low Tig

✧ "Somebody goes het, and you've just to be up high and they can't tig ye. Low Tig's the same idea, only ye bend doun."

Hopping Tig

✧ Also called "Hoppie Tig." A game in which the one that's het has to hop on one foot and so have all the rest to hop.

Hospital Tig

✧ "This is my favourite tig. Wherever you're tigged—on the eye, on the heid, or the airm, or on the leg, you've to hold that part with one hand as though you were hurt, and ye've to go about like that and try to tig somebody else."

Lame Tig

✧ "Everybody playin' must limp wi' one leg, and so has the one that's het."

Leapfrog Tig

✧ Similar to Tunnel Tig, except that you are freed from being tigged by your playmates leaping over your bended back.

Linie Tig

✧ "We used to chase each other round the playground, but our feet must not move off the painted lines used for tennis or netball."

Pirates' Tig

✧ Played in the swing-park. One person is het and keeps running round the set of swings, hoping and endeavouring to tig someone swinging to the side he's passing. On the ground, right underneath each swing, is a white square on which the swinger must not rest his feet. The one that's het is forbidden to pass between the swings, an offence which is described as "cutting the cheese."

This game is played as readily by girls as by boys, and similar games in these parks make use of the see-saw and the merry-go-round.

Plain Tig

✧ Otherwise known as "Ordinary Tig," this starts with the simple action of tigging, along with the statement "Tig, you're het," after which the tigger runs away.

Pole Tig

✧ "Ye can have about four people playing. They all claim a pole in the back-green, and the one that's out stands in the middle, shuts their eyes and counts up to ten. When she opens her eyes, she tries to get a pole that's empty or tig someone running between."

Another way of playing is for the person that's het to cry out "Change!" and then count up to ten before opening her eyes. Instead of "Change!" you can call out "Jump!" or "Run!" or "Hop!" or "Bunny jump!" or "Skip!" or "Twirl!" or "Scissors!" or "Umbrellas!" and it is according to these orders that the players have to move between the poles. "Scissors!" refers to a cross-step that has to be made, and "Umbrellas!" means that you have to walk pretending to be carrying an umbrella.

Scabbie Touch

- "Ye get plenty o' people and you find a piece o' rag, some scabbie-lookin' thing, that's the joke, and ye play at tig, and ye throw it at a person, and if it touches them they're het."

Shadow Tig

- "It's got to be a sunny day. Ye've to try and step on another person's shadow. And if ye step on a person's shadow, they're het. If there's a shadow cast by a building, the person who you're chasin' can run into it and that counts as a den."

Sheepdog Tig

- The first person tigged is put into the den and as the game goes on and more are tigged they can join the sheepdog—so long as one sheep is left in the den (or fold).

Shoelace Tig

- "Somebody goes het, and after he tigs some one that person has to lowse [loosen] both his laces, then he has to tie them up again, and chase after the rest."

Siver Tig

- "Any number can play. Ye a' run to a siver [grating over a street gutter drain] and ye're safe there until the one that's out cries 'Change!' or 'Budge!' and ye've to run to another siver, and when ye're runnin' the one that's out tries to tig you."

Square Tig

- "This is a game for five. Four o' them form a square and try to swop corners wi' each other. The one that's het stands in the middle and tries tae nab a corner so that somebody else'll have to go het."

Sticky Toffee

- "Ye a' stand, it's just like tig, but when the one that's het comes up to you, ye bend doun on your knees and shout 'Sticky toffee!' and they cannie tig ye. But sometimes ye get co't [caught]. Three tigs and ye go het."

Torchie Tig

- "This is what we play. Say ye have three torches. Then three volunteers go het and the rest go and hide, and efter counting up to five hundred maybe, the three wi' the torches go and look for the rest—ye ken it's a dark night when ye play. The last three to be caught, tug that is, are het for the next game because everybody wants a shot o' the torches, and if it was the first three everybody would try to get tug first."

Tunnel Tig

✧ "If you are tigged, you have to stand with your legs apart, but your chums can free you by diving under your legs. The person who's het has to tig everybody, and when everybody's standing with their legs apart, the person first tigged is het for the next game."

In another type of tunnel tig the tunnel or arch is formed by placing one hand or both hands against a wall or lamp-post.

White Tig

✧ You play this running along a road. You can't be tigged if you stand on anything that's white. There's a widish interpretation of what's white—some bits of the pavement are looked on as white, nearby portions being darker.

Windmill Tig

✧ "The person that's het stands with their back to the other folk wi' arms waving up and down. The other folk have to run and get under these arms without being touched. If they are, they have to join the person that's out and start waving their arms too."

HIDE-AND-SEEK

"I was," wrote Robert Louis Stevenson, "the best player of hide-and-seek going: not a good runner, I was up to every shift and dodge, I could jink very well, I could crawl without any noise through leaves, I could hide under a carrot plant: it used to be my favourite boast that I always walked into the den."

In "Hide-and-Seek" (also called "Hessy"[1] or "Hide and Go Seek" or "Hidie-go" or "I Spy") the person who's het has to shut their eyes and count up to a certain number to give the

---

[1] "Hessy" comes from "Hespy" which comes from "Hi-spy." Scott knew the game as "Hy-Spy." "I must come to play Blind Harry and Hy-Spy . . ." *Guy Mannering* (1815).

others time to hide. The counting can, however, be done in fives ("Five, ten, fifteen, twenty . . .") or even in tens ("Ten, twenty, thirty, forty . . ."). Yet another way of counting is:

✦   Five, ten, double ten,
       Five, ten, fifty:
       Five, ten, double ten,
       Five, ten a hundred.

Over the years this version has got condensed into:

✦   Five, ten, double ten,
       Five, ten, a hundred.

The arithmetic is faulty but the result comes quicker, especially if you have to count up to five hundred or more.

To allow the hiders time to run away and conceal themselves how many hundreds has the seeker to count up to ?

✦ "Say theres' eight playin', ye count four for the den, that's twelve, so it's twelve hundred ye count up tae."

✦ "If there's five playin', that's five to start wi', six" (points up to the sky), "seven" (points down to the ground), "eight" (points east), "nine" (points west). "That means ye count up to nine hundred."

✦ "We do one for the wall and one for the person and one for luck!"

✦ "We coont 'pole-one, pole-two' . . . right up to 'pole-fifteen.' Either that or we start 'coco-fifteen, coco-fourteen' . . . and go down to 'coco-one'."

✦ "We do the 'Snake.' Take the lassie that's het, ye draw a snake on her back wi' your finger, twice, and ye're sayin':

       Draw the snake
       Draw the snake
       Guess which finger touched?

Ye see ye touch the snake. Actually ye gie [give] her a right poke in the back and ye hud [hold] up the fingers o' your hand spread oot, so that when she whips roond, she picks the one that done it. If she guesses right she jist coonts to a hundred, if she guesses wrong she picks another finger . . . And it goes

E

on like that. Since ye have jist five fingers on one hand, the maist she'll ever have to coont up tae is five hundred."

Some players say:

> "I draw the snake
> Upon your back
> Which finger dared to touch?"

And the snake is sometimes called "a curly-wurly snake."

Once the game is started the first spied is always the next het. And when this player has been discovered the cry is raised:

> ✧ Come oot, come oot, wherever you are
> For Jenny Wilson's het!

If, in her turn, Jenny Wilson is a bit slow in seeking out the other players, or is looking in the wrong direction, one of the hidden can call out:

> ✧ Come oot, come oot, ya hungry hen
> And look for a' your chickens!

Very often what happens is that the seeker calls out, "I spy Mary Maclennan!" And the said Mary Maclennan cries back, "That was Hetty Turnbull's heid [head] ye saw movin', —no mine!" And of course there's a disagreement. If the rest of the players side with the seeker, and Mary Maclennan won't appear to take her shot of being het, then the players chorus out:

> ✧ She'll no come oot!
> She'll no come oot!
> The game's stuck up!
> The game's 'stuck up!

Or:

> ✧ The gemm's stuck up!
> The gemm's stuck up,
> A' through Mary Maclennan!

Other calling chants to bring the players out of hiding are:

> ✧ Come oot, come oot,
> Wherever ye are:

The ^aBogey's in   ^a *goblin, devil*
The ^bjeely jar!   ^b *jelly*

- ◇   . . . The game's up the pole! (or spout!)

- ◇   . . . The game's doun the drain!

- ◇   . . . The game's a bogey!

There are over half a dozen forms of "Hide-and-Seek":

Buses

◇   Also called "Turn-the-Wheel." Someone goes to the end of the street to see if a certain bus or make of car is coming while the rest of the players hide. When the bus or car appears, that's the signal for returning to seek out the others. "I'm no waiting on a Cadillac, mind [remember]!"

I Spread the Butter

◇   "The person who's het stands with his back to the others who say:

> I spread the butter
> I spread the cheese
> I spread the jam
> On your dirty knees—
> Guess who touched!

Now supposing the person guesses Sylvia, the rest ask, 'What has she to do?' 'Run to the top o' the street, count sixty and come back.' And Sylvia does this while we hide, but if it wasnie Sylvia at all we say, 'Do it yoursel'!' and then we hide."

"This is how we play it. After asking, 'Who touched?' maybe he guesses Willie and it was really me. O.K. 'How many fish are in a barrel?' 'Three.' And what he says Willie has to do he has to do it hissel [himself] three times. And we hide." Another question often put to get a number is: "How many eggs are in a bush?"

Kick the Can

◇   Otherwise known as "Tin-Can Tommy." You start off by throwing the can away, and the person who's het retrieves it and replaces it in the den, hiding his eyes and counting up to an agreed number. The other players hide. When anyone is spied there's a race to the can, which the spier must touch before the other can kick it. On many occasions the one that's spied is too far off to make a race of it, and so the spier can almost amble back to the den. Even then he's pretty canny and careful and as though addressing the can, he taps it gently with his toe and says in an undertone "No kick the can!" or "No kick the can, one two three!" The ones caught stay in the den —but the last man can free all. When the can is kicked the shout of "Kick the can!" goes up triumphantly.

Robinson Crusoe

✧ The one that's het sings out, in any place where he may think his playmates are hiding:

> Robinson Crusoe
> Give us a call:
> Give us an answer
> Or not at all!

If they are within earshot, one of them is bound to reply, "Pee-weep! Pee-weep!" And if the one that's het guesses the crier's name correctly, he or she must come out of concealment. The favourite hiding-place for this game are the flats and half-flats of tenement stairways.

Sardines

✧ "First we toss up to see who's to hide. The hiding-place in this game has to be fairly big to hold a number of hiders. Then everybody shuts their eyes and counts till this one person gets away. He or she then hides, and the seekers set out to look for him or her. They can't go in pairs. When they spy the hiding one, they first make sure that none of the others is watching them and they slip in beside the hider and more and more do this until all are packed in the hiding-place like sardines in a tin. The first to find the first hider hides first in the next game."

Ten Wee Sodgers

✧ "Say there was a boy, he turns his back and hides his eyes. Then one of us puts their hand on his back and we go:

> Ten wee sodgers [soldiers] marching up the hill:
> The officer cried, 'Halt! Who touched?'

And somebody touches him and he turns round and guesses who; and say he says it was me, well if it wasnie me the one that it was wouldnie let on, and so he'd go on, 'You run over to so-and-so place'; and when he's finished speaking he has to do it himself if it wasnie me, and when he's doing the running the rest of us hide and he's to come and look for us. The first spied is het unless he's freed—ye see there's a den and we play 'Last man frees all'."

Twenty-a-Lespie

"The person that's het shuts their eyes and counts down from 'twenty-a-lespie,' and everybody else runs away and hides. Everybody hidden has to be caught and the first caught is the next het. If nobody's caught the same person that's het has to shut their eyes again and this time counts from Nineteen-a-lespie. And so on."

"Forty Buzz Off" is the same game, only you count down from "forty" instead of "twenty."

Water Water Wallflower

This game is played by girls. The one who's het (say she's called Alice Henderson) stands with her back to a wall, and the rest line up in front of her and sing:

> Water water wallflower
> Growing up so high
> We are all maidens
> And we must all die:
> Except Alice Henderson
> For she's the fondest lover
> She can dance and she can sing
> And she can lick the sugar:
>
> Fie fie fie for shame—
> Turn your face to the wall again!

At the proper moment they all point at Alice Henderson. She turns her face to the wall, and while the others scatter and go into hiding she counts, "Five, ten, fifteen, twenty . . .," up to an agreed number. Then she may add:

> Here I come, away or not
> By one, by two, by three!

"Water Water Wallflower" is less played nowadays. In an older version the second verse ends:

> . . . She can dance and she can sing
> And she shall wear the wedding ring.

Finally, here is an old story. "Two boys going to play Hide and Seek, one called himself Trouble, the other called himself Mind-your-own-business. This one hid his eyes, and when he started to look for his friend here he met a Bobbie [policeman], who stopped him and asked him: 'What's your name?'— 'Mind-your-own-business.'—'What are you looking for?'— 'Trouble.' "

4

BOOLS, PEERIES, KNIFIE, AND SUCH-LIKE

Nearly all the Scots, born in Edinburgh, who have distinguished themselves in literature or science were brought up on our traditional games. Scott, Stevenson, Clerk Maxwell, all played them. When he attended Edinburgh Academy Clerk Maxwell seldom took part in "school" games. But "Bools"[1] and "Peeries"[2] were a different matter. His imagination revelled in all these collisions and gyrations!

BOOLS

"Bools [marbles]" is a game played in the springtime when the days start to lengthen out. The bools are of various sizes and may be made of clay, glass, or steel. Nowadays they are mostly "glessies [glasses]." "Chuckies," "hoggies," and "dollickers" are all extra-big bools. A "cat's eye" is a big glass bool "with a wee bit colour in the middle." So is a "bull's eye" or a "Chinese checker." "Cherries" are glass bools of a white-and-red colour. "Clayies" and "peas" are the ordinary bools in different self-colours, and "steelies" are ball-bearings. A "placer" is "a wee bool that ye put doun in place of a bigger one so that it's more difficult to hit." A "plonker [knuckler]" is the bool that you're hitting with. You can also call it a "rollie." A "plonk" is "an in-between bool, a glessie o' different colours." Every boy likes to keep his bools in a "boolie bag." They're safer that way!

> ◇ "If some laddies are cooryin' roond [huddling round] playin' bools, and ye steal a handfie [handful] in the passin', and ye cry 'Puggie,' that means ye're no a thief!"

[1] Fr. *boule*, ball.
[2] A peg-top shaped like a "peer [pear]."

Here are a dozen or so different games of bools.

Holie

✧ Also called "Plonkie." "In this game ye make a hole in the
ground and ye a' stand in a line a good wee bit away and ye
fire [throw] the bools to see who can get the nearest. The
nearest gets the first chance to roll into the hole. If he misses, it's
the next nearest and so on. Whoever gets in takes a 'plonk
[knuckled shot]' at any o' the other bools. If he hits this one,
he lifts it up, it's his, and he rolls back into the hole and then
tries a shot at another bool. Whenever he misses, the next
nearest gets the roll-up to the hole. Anybody whose bool has
been hit and lifted is out the game or he can join in and roll up
any time if the rest of the players agree. The player whose bool
is being aimed at does 'keppie [catch]' with his feet. He stands
either wi' heels touching or huddin' [holding] the inside of his
foot at right angles to the shot. For 'Chinese keppie' he turns
his back and points his toes together—the bool lies in the angle.
When plonking the bool, the knuckle of the forefinger must
be touching on the edge of the hole. A 'pussie' or a 'cattie' is a
shot that's pushed and no right 'plonked [knuckled].' If the
bool's got stanes in front o' it or any other obstruction ye can
claim 'heights,' either 'low heights' or 'high heights.' That
means you can aim your shot fae [from] high up. Some cry it
'highie' or 'kneeie,' meaning, fae your knee. If your bool's
awfie [awfully] close to the hole so that the one that's aimin'
can hardly miss, ye can ask for 'backie'—he has to plonk from
the back of the hole or ye can ask for 'blindie,' he has to aim
from the front of the hole—but his eyes must be shut."

　　If your opponent's bool is behind a pole or a wall you shout
"Rounds!" and he has to bring it from behind the obstacle into
the open, unless, of course, he has first shouted "Nae rounds!"
If one bool is plonked at another and misses and rolls far away,
the next player in the hole can shout "Nearies!"—in which
case the owner of the far away bool has to bring it nearer. He
has the right to place it anywhere near, but he doesn't do a
thing if he has first shouted "Nae nearies!" When the ground
is earthy and very level, making your bool an easy target, you
cry "Grounders!"—which allows you to stamp your bool into
the ground. But not if the cry "Nae grounders!" has been
raised! Sometimes, if you are in the hole and ready to plonk,
you can first hit one bool, then without rolling back, you can
elect to plonk from there and hit a second, and so on. But you

must earlier have cried "Pairs!" or "Trebles!" or "Quads!"
Some players hit the bools in this fashion, only they cry
"Clecks!" each time. But all these ideas can be forestalled by
your opponent—"Nae pairs!" "Nae trebles!" or "Nae
quads!" or "Nae clecks!" or "Nae backie!" or "Nae blindie!"

The rules that you play to must be agreed at the beginning
of the game. "No rebounds!" means you can't rebound into
the hole off a keppie. "No back hits" means that the bool must
be hit cleanly. But such could be allowed if agreed on. A hit
on a bool "off a wall" can also count or not. If, in plonking, a
player by mistake hits a second bool after hitting the first, the
cry of "Cannons!" goes up, and he loses two bools. Some say
"Hit two, pay two." A cry of "Fans!" "Fannies!" or "Chinese
fans!" establishes the right to wave the sole of your shoe rapidly
to and fro while your opponent takes his aim. This distracts
him. There are also a number of whigmaleeries [foolish
fancies] that may be uttered from time to time. "Hookie
pookie, make you miss!" or "Issie issie, cat's missie!" or (after
making a cross with your forefinger):

> Monkey's cross
> 'll make ye [a]loss!   [a] *lose*

—which is usually countered with

> Elephant's skin
> 'll make me win!

Or your foe may come out with

> Chinese cross
> Make him [a]loss!   [a] *lose*

—while your pal prays

> Banana skin
> Make him win!

There are, of course, other ways of hitting the bool besides
plonking it. If you shout "Rollie!" you can place the bool at
the top of your palm, hold it there with one finger, and then
by slanting your palm, you let it roll down and hit the other
bool. And if the laddie whose bool is being aimed at happens
to say "Chinese choppers!" you must lift your bool high in
the air above his, and then you let go in the hope of smacking
it.

At the very start of the game, besides throwing the bool towards the hole, the players may choose to plonk it or do a "snakie," which is a special way of pitching the bool. "Baggie first shot!" or "Baggie first!" leads off, and "if ye want to play last, ye shout 'Laggie!'" And supposing in this roll-up two bools actually drop into the hole together, what happens? Either the two players roll again or one of them shouts "Kisses!" or "Chuckies!"

"The two bools are then shaken in your hand, chucked up in the air and let land. The nearest the hole gets the first shot but, the other man has the right to the second shot." A favourite bool for using in a "rollie [roll-up]" is a steelie, because its weight carries it better over bumpy ground. Provided you're not barred by "Nae swoppies!" you may change your bool at any moment. And, if the bool slips as you're preparing to plonk, "Slips!" allows you to retake the shot—unless you're beaten to it by "Nae slips!" And lastly, "if we've got just a wee drop bools we play at 'funny' and no 'keepie'."

Bartering of bools takes place more during off-periods, but in this business the playing reputation of certain bools isn't forgotten: "I gien [gave] Smidgers [Smith] seven clayies for his 'lucky yin [one].'"

Stakie

✧ Also called "Ringie" or "Daikie." On the ground you chalk or scratch a ring, into which all the players put an equal share of bools. The size of the ring varies with the number of bools and the number of players. Then everybody stands about four or five feet away, and each rolls one bool and the nearest to the ring gets first plonk at the bools inside. If this player knocks one bool out of the ring, he keeps it. If he knocks two out, then before any of the others can say "Knock out two, put one back," he says "Knock out two, put none back," and keeps both. And the same applies to three or more. When he misses, the next nearest gets the chance of plonking, and when all the "daik [deck, staked bools]" is finished, a fresh game is started.

In the roll-up at the beginning, someone is bound to shout "First knocks!" which is followed by claims of "Second knocks!" and so on. If two or more players roll into the ring or touch the ring, then this calling settles the order of plonking. Incidentally, the ring is nearly always referred to as the "hole." And "In Musselburgh the name we give to the 'roll-up' is the 'trow.'"

Chinese Checkers

❖ Also called "Plonkers" or "Bombers." Another ring game. "Ye roll for first shot," and the winner lets his bool fall from above to try to knock as many bools as possible out the ring. Those he knocks out he keeps. The big "cat's eye" is a favourite "bomber." An "eye drop" is a shot let fall from under your eye.

Dowsie

❖ "A hollow was made between the causey-stanes and all the players, usually about half a dozen, played up to this hole. All the players in turn then took a shot at the bool that lay furthest from the hole with the idea of sending it in the direction of the nearest siver. When everybody had had a bash, the owner of this bool was then allowed one throw back to the hole. If he failed to get in, the bashing of his bool went on until either it was dowsed doun the siver or else he saved himself by getting into the hole."

Fat

❖ This was a boolie game played in Leith and round about, in the 1920s. We rolled up to the lid of a street hydrant that was oblong in shape. The one whose bool was nearest decided the tunk [stake] that each player then put on to the lid. For this purpose we had a scale of values. It went:

> 2 commons = 1 cheenie or 1 cat's eye
>
> 2 cheenies = 1 wee glessie.

Commons were a brown, oatmealie colour, a cheenie [china] was white with a glazed finish and the value of any glessie depended on its size and colouring. A plunker was a big glessie. In this game the lowest bool was a common, and although 2 peas = 1 common, we didn't allow play with peas. A pea was a lassie's bool!

After the tunk had been placed, the one nearest then got first shot and his aim was to knock out of the lid as many bools as possible. These he collected. On no account had his bool to remain on the lid. In the course of the play if it did remain he had to replace not only those he had knocked out on that occasion but also all those he had already won—in the same game. The one nearest the hole if he chose could "bull up," that is, miss his shot but the next time his turn came round he had the right of plunking from the edge of the lid.

"Bull up" means of course "bool up," the word "bull" being pronounced to rhyme with "dull."

Gutterie

❖ You roll the bools along the gutter, and the idea is to keep your opponent's bool always in front of yours, in which case you're allowed to plonk it. For every two hits that you are "up," he has to hand over a bool. If there are stones, leaves, or rubbish obscuring your opponent's bool, you have to cry "Clearie!" before he shouts "No clearies!" There are a number of other privileges that you must claim before he bars them: when your bool's caught in a crack, "Ups!"; when it's on the high road or a pavement, "Downs!"; and when it's rolling on too far, and you're in front of the other player, "Stops!" In "Gutterie" there are no keppies except where there's a "siver [drain-cover]."

With many gutters being rather dangerous to play along, this game is carried on in safer areas under the name of "Chasie."

Lampie

❖ This was greatly played from Victorian times right up to the 1920s. Nowadays it's quite out of vogue. To start, you didn't knuckle the bool, you threw it against the base of a lamp-post. Your opponent followed suit, and if his rebound touched your bool, he collared it. If he missed, then you struck the lamp-post with another bool, and if this time you scored a hit on one of the bools, then you collected both. With a lot of misses quite a lot of bools gathered in the kitty—for someone to win!

Knickelie

❖ "As many people can play as ye want. Ye a' roll your bools and the nearest to the hole is the first to try and 'knickle [knuckle]' his bool into the hole. If he gets in he next tries to knickle any o' the other bools into the hole. To 'knickle' means to strike the bool wi' the nail o' your thumb as it springs fae [from] the point o' your forefinger. The bools that the laddie knickles in, he 'sticks tae [keeps].' If he misses, the nearest the hole gets a shot."

Linie

❖ In Portobello this was the game we liked best and played most. "Colourts [coloureds, glessies]" were the bools we played for, but the bools we played with, came chiefly from the bottle works—they formed the stoppers in the necks of bottles of fizz [lemonade]. Colourts were given the name of "liners," according to their size. The smallest were quarter or half-liners and the biggest might be a three-liner. If it was your shot you put your colourt down on the pavement on the line where the flagstones met, and the other laddies fired their bools at it in turn. If your bool was a two-liner, they aimed from two lines away and so on. When they missed, you kept their bools, but if some boy hit your colourt, he claimed it, and now it was his chance to put down his colourt.

"Stope [stop] smoolyin'" was what we cried when some one edged over the proper line of fire, and a player who pushed instead of knuckling the bool was called "a pushie Nellie."

Monkey Chips

◇ A bool is put into a hole and then from an agreed distance the players in turn throw a bigger bool at it and try to chip it.

Rowie

◇ "You have a big long line o' bools in a row, and ye plonk at them and try to get as many oot [out of] the line as ye can. The ones ye get oot, ye keep. Ye aye [always] plonk from where your bool happens to stop. And if ye miss, somebody else has a try. When your turn comes roond again, ye start from where ye last were."

Wallie

◇ You roll towards a wall and the nearest to the wall gets the first plonk at the others. There are no keppies in wallie.

Boolie Banker

◇ "You've got a cardboard box and ye make big holes and wee holes till they get doun to the size o' a bool, and then ye write numbers above the holes, above the big ones maybe one or nothing, and above the wee ones five or six, and then ye've got a man that acts as a kind o' banker, and he's got to have a lot o' bools and then ye take your shots in turn, and ye try to get them into the best hole, and ye win the number o' bools that's written on the top o' the hole. The bools that go into nothing or dinnie go into any o' the holes, the banker collects."

PEERIES

Virgil's "Arma virumque cano . . ." must have bored Clerk Maxwell, for at the age of thirteen he wrote a poem which began:

Of pearies and their origin I sing. . . .

"Peeries"—those fascinating pear-shaped tops[3] were once almost too plentiful on the city pavements. Not today. Yet the peerie still birls [spins] cheerfully in the quieter back streets. It is usually wound with string, and it spins on a pointed metal foot. Once started, it is very often whipped about. The whip consists of a stick with a long leather lash. When the peerie falls over it's "deid [dead]," and when it's spinning motionless it is said to be "dozing." A humming-top was called a "French peerie." Boys of an older generation loved to decorate their peeries with chalk so that each spun with a coat of many colours, or wove circles or spirals.

Between players the game very often is to see who can spin his peerie longest. But whipping-games are the most popular.

Racing Peeries
◇ A boy races his peerie against his friend's.

Goals
◇ "You make two goals and you have three or four a side and each side tries to whip the peerie through the other goal."

Sides
◇ "In the playground or back-green you draw a boundary line about eight feet long, and ye pick sides, but no too many, and one side has the peerie, and they've to try and whip it across the boundary line, and the other side have to try and keep it out. When they get it over, if they do, the other side gets a shot o' attacking instead o' defending. The side that gets the peerie across the line in the shortest time wins."

[3] Both "la toupie [top]" and "la boule [ball]" furnished Baudelaire with imagery for his poetry; and the French peerie must, indirectly, have suggested the line: "Comme un Ange cruel qui fouette des soleils." *Le Voyage* (1861).

KNIFIE

As its name implies, "Knifie" is played with a knife, and there are at least three different forms of it:

- One of the older games of knifie began with each player throwing his knife so that it stuck either in the ground or on a deal table-top. You had to perform this thrice, otherwise you couldn't properly begin the real game. In this game, one hand, usually the left hand, was placed flat on the ground or on the table with the fingers spread out like a fan. The point of the knife was then played in and out the spaces between the fingers. There was a regular series of patterns you had to follow and the winner was the person who accomplished this quickest— and without making a mistake. In making a mistake you were liable to cut or at least jag yourself.

- In the game that's called 'knifie' nowadays, two laddies stand facing each other, each with his two feet close together. Each gets a shot with the knife, turn about, and the idea is to stick the knife in the ground or on the floor within a foot's length of your opponent's shoe. If the knife lands further off than this, it doesn't count. You also play to the left shoe and to the right shoe alternately. Each player, after each knife-throw, must move his foot up to where the knife has stuck, and in this way the legs get spread further and further apart until at last one of the players finds it impossible to stand up. He therefore loses the game. If, in the throw, the knife lands between your opponent's feet, then the next throw must be aimed backwards over the shoulder.

- In another form of the game, "ye're always trying to stick the point of the knife into the mud or soft ground. Ye start off wi' the knife lying balanced across the back o' your hand and ye flick it free, to let it fall. After the back of your hand, the order is: the back o' your finger (any finger), the point o' your toe (foot lifted off the ground), the cap o' your raised knee, the edge o' your hip, the end o' your raised elbow, the top o' your shoulder, the bridge o' your nose, the cleft o' your chin, and lastly the top o' your brow (tilted back). At any bit [stage] when ye fail, somebody else gets a shot. Sometimes ye play for ha'pennies."

DIABOLO

"Diabolo" has never been completely forgotten, and it still has occasional revivals. An old name is "The Devil on Two Sticks," and Clerk Maxwell mentions it in a letter he wrote in 1848—when he was seventeen:

> ❧ I have been reading Xenophon's *Memorabilia* after breakfast. . . . Then a game of the Devil of whom there is a duality and a quaternity of sticks so that I can play either conjunctly or severally. I can jump over him and bring him round without leaving go the sticks. I can also keep him up behind me.

Maxwell had also a great habit of referring to the diabolo in a very affectionate undertone as "The Deil!"

Nowadays girls play this game much more than boys do but outstanding performers are few and far between. The grandmothers of today remember the game well and claim that they were very accomplished: "That's true. I mind fine I could send it higher than the tenements and catch it, back and front. I could dae 'double decker' as well and put it through baith my airms and my legs."

CAT'S CRADLES

Along with bools, peeries, and diabolo, Clerk Maxwell was greatly devoted to these "Cat's Cradles." He even wrote a "(Cat's) Cradle Song" of which here are two verses:

> Clear your coil of kinkings
>   Into perfect plaiting
> Locking loops and linkings
>   Interpenetrating.
>
> It's monstrous, horrid, shocking
>   Beyond the power of thinking
> Not to know interlocking
>   Is no mere form of linking.

Popular figures are "Tallow Candles," "See-saw," "Piggie Goes to Market" and, in particular, the "Forth Bridge."

CHUCKIES

In the back-greens of the 1900s, 1910s, and 1920s, "Chuckies" was considered the ideal game for a warm summer's day, and the best pitch the stone landing of an "outside stairway." The chuckies, four in number, were generally coloured red, blue, green, and yellow. They were cube-shaped with four sides, fluted. They were sold in a sort of big matchbox, and along with them was supplied a rather large "bool"—a "dollicker," in fact. This dollicker was meant to be stotted [bounced] during the progress of the game, but the players (usually girls) preferred to use a small rubber ball:

Chuckies

✧ In the *first round*, the four chuckies are placed in a square-like fashion:

2 3
1 4

Then—meanwhile performing the actions noted—you chant the following verses:

WORDS	LEFT HAND	RIGHT HAND
Sweep the flair [floor]	*Stot ball and catch it.*	*Wave flatly above Chuckie No. 1.*
Lift one chair	*Same.*	*Pick up Chuckie No. 1.*
Sweep below	*Same.*	*Wave above Chuckie No. 2, and pick it up.*
And lay it there:	*Same.*	*Put down Chuckies Nos. 1 and 2 where No. 1 was to begin with.*
Sweep the flair	*Same.*	*Wave flatly above Chuckies Nos. 1 and 2.*
Lift two chairs	*Same.*	*Pick up Chuckies Nos. 1 and 2.*
Sweep below	*Same.*	*Wave above Chuckie No. 3, and pick it up.*
And lay them there.	*Same.*	*Put down Chuckies Nos. 1, 2, and 3 where No. 1 was to begin with.*

F

Similarly for "three chairs" and then "four chairs"—which leaves all four chuckies where the first one was to begin with. Each time the ball is stotted, it must be caught, otherwise the player is out: but having successfully accomplished all the actions already mentioned, the player then "goes down the scale," restoring each of the chuckies to its original position.

At the beginning of the *second round*, all four chuckies are scattered, and they are finally returned to a scattered position: but in all other respects, the second round follows the same procedure as the first. With a lot of sweeping, the players' hands get rubbed quite smooth and tender.

In the *third round*, the chuckies are placed squarely; and, very much in a counting-out fashion, the player, ball in hand, goes round each of the chuckies in turn with the ball, while chanting a rhyme like "My wee Jeanie" or "Cross the Railway by the Bridge Only." Above the chuckie at which the rhyme stops, the player throws the ball up into the air, picks up that chuckie, and catches the ball. The player then repeats the line, picks up the chuckie at which it stops, throws up the ball, with both chuckies, and catches them—and so on, until all four chuckies have been picked up. Finally the player goes down the scale, and restores all four chuckies to their original positions.

In the *fourth round*, the chuckies are placed on top of each other forming a little tower. The ball is bounced, the topmost chuckie lifted, and the ball caught. Then the ball is bounced a second time, the next chuckie snatched, and the ball caught. Meanwhile the tower musn't be knocked over. After the chuckies have been lifted one at a time, two at a time are tackled, then three and one, and lastly the whole four. In the same way the tower is rebuilt, playing the game backwards.

In the *fifth round*, the ball is thrown up or bounced with one hand, and the same hand picks up and throws up one chuckie. The ball is then caught in the same hand and the chuckie is caught on the back of the other hand. Next two chuckies are thrown up and caught, then three, and finally four. After this feat the game is played down the scale.

Nowadays the game of chuckies is seldom so fully played. In the past the game had many other variations of its rituals not noted here. Sometimes no ball is used and a fifth chuckie takes its place—to be thrown in the air when necessary. This is the game most popular today. Square-shaped stones are often played with, when proper chuckies are not available.

"Jackies" or "Ball and Jack" and "Fivestones" are all similar to Chuckies.

PAIPS

Paips

✧ A summer game of long ago, played with cherry-stones.[4] You counted your "paips [pips]" or stones in castles or "caddles"[5] of four. A small hole was made in the ground and the players in turn tried to pitch a caddle of paips into the hole. Each stood about four paces away. The player who got the most paips into the hole scooped the lot. Laddies and lassies would brag about the number of caddles they'd either won at paips or amassed after eating cherries!

Paipie

✧ "This is what we played in Stockaree during the cherry season. A small bed was marked out with skilly [slate pencil] either on the pavement or on the concrete of the playground:

You poodled up your paip and if it entered a square with a number you got that number of paips from the banker. The banker collected all the misses. To 'poodle' means to push forward your paip. Usually this was done by squeezing it between the forefinger and the thumb, and the poodler stood or more frequently knelt about a couple of feet away from the squares."

Paips (and plum-stones) were often played with instead of buttons in the game of Buttonie.

[4] James Ballantine, *The Auld West Port* (1843):

The bools, paips and piries and a' siccan sport
Were aye played wi' birr in the auld West Port

[5] Fr. *quartelle*.

Tossing Pennies

When youngsters are seen in corners either playing cards or tossing coins,[6] it is nearly always assumed that they are more interested in gambling than in the theory of probability. It is this assumption which gives a thrill to these games.

Pitch & Toss

✧ The players stand at an agreed distance from a wall. You hold your penny in the palm of your hand and throw it openly to get as near to the wall as possible. The one that's nearest wins all the pennies that have been pitched and tossed.

Odd Man Out

✧ "There's three o' yez wi' pennies and yez a' toss them up— 'Birl up!'—and catch them flat in one palm, coverin' quickly wi' the other palm. Then ye show up. Whaever's 'Odd man out' wins the pennies. If it's three heids [heads] or three tails, ye toss again."

Heading

✧ "You throw two pennies up in the air, and if they come doun two heids [heads], you keep them. If they come doun two tails you pay double. Heid and tail, you toss again. To begin with you lay the pennies tails upward on the palm of your hand and you flick them up so that they turn in the air."

Headman Guesses

✧ "Well, say there's jist you and me, and you toss your penny and I toss mine, supposing you got a heid and I got a tail, I toss my penny again, and you guess. If you guess right, you keep the penny, if ye guess wrong, I keep it."

Odds & Evens

✧ "You toss your penny, and I toss mine. You show up, a tail maybe, and if ye think mine's a tail, ye shout 'Evens!' but if ye think it's a heid ye shout 'Odds!' If ye guess correct, ye get the penny."

[6] James Ballantine, *The Wee Raggit Laddie* (1843):

| At bools thou nicks, at paips thou [a]praps | [a]aim, strike |
| Thou birls bawbees, thou dozes taps . . . | (Fr. *frapper*) |

CARD-GAMES

There are a few card-games not too well known to need description.

Stop the Bus

⟡ You're dealt three cards each and they must add up to 31. That stops the bus.

Snap

⟡ "You each get half the pack and turn the cards up one at a time and in turn until you get two the same and the first to ay 'Snap!' wins them."

White Horse

⟡ "You a' get three cards each and ye a' keep lifting off the rest o' the pack till ye get a run, then ye shout 'White Horse!' and take the kitty. If ye keep quiet and somebody shouts 'White Horse!' and your hand is higher than theirs, then ye not only collect the kitty, but ye take double money off the person."

Strip Jack Naked

⟡ "If three play you deal three cards and whaeever's got the lowest takes something off, and the game goes on until somebody is stripped naked."

Haymarket

⟡ "Ye take the four Kings oot [out] the pack and pit [put] them on the table. They're the four horses, and ye put a ha'penny in the kitty and whatever ye want on any o' the horses.

Ye deal the pack oot, and say there's three folk playin', ye deal four hands, and the person that has the double hand, if he looks at yin [one] o' thae [these] hands and lays it aside then he's stuck wi' the other.

Ace o' Spades starts and on it goes the two o' Spades, the three, and so on, and whaeever cannie [can't] play a Spade he must jist [just] play any low red card and the rest follie [follow], and whaeever comes up wi' any Queen, he takes what's on that King, and the yin that first has nae cairds left, he lifts the kitty."

Scabbie Annie

❖ Otherwise called "The Scabbie Queen": "Ye get a pack o' cairds [cards] and ye take one caird oot [withoot lookin' at it) and then ye deal the remainder and efter they're a' dealt, each player has to make as many pairs as possible and so ye get goin' clockwise, somebody picks a caird from your hand and you pick a caird fae [from] his—to get pairs, see. The pairs are laid oot in the middle o' the table, and when a' the cairds are oot, there's one fellie [fellow] left wi' the odd caird. That's 'Scabbie Annie' or the 'Scabbie Queen' and the fellie gets ducked."

Trumph

❖ "Five people's the most that can play. Ye deal seven cards each and when you've dealt the last card oot, ye turn the tope [top] card over to see what's to be trumph—ayther [either] Hearts, Shovels, Curlies or Diamonds. The dealer lays a card doun first and the others follow suit and the highest or the trumph wins. Then six cards are dealt, and efter that five and so on. The ones that dinnie win a single set they should be oot the gemm [game] but they get 'a dug's [dog's] chance.' This means that in the next round they get one caird only and they can come in when they like unless they're forced tae. Whaever wins the last gemm when two cairds each is dealt, that yin ca's [calls] the trump when only one caird is dealt."

SALOON-GAMES

Schoolboys playing snooker or billiards are apt to get classed among the riff-raff or among the cads (like Coker[7] of the Fifth in *The Magnet*). Yet our best philosopher wrote: "Here is a billiard ball lying on the table and another ball moving towards it with rapidity. They strike: and the ball which was formerly at rest, now acquires motion. This is as perfect an instance of the relation between cause and effect as any which we know.... Let us therefore examine it." This examination introduced perhaps the greatest discovery ever made in pure thinking: that there is no connexion between cause and effect except as experienced in our minds. It's amusing to imagine that David

---

[7] Character in school stories written by Frank Richards (1875-1962), the creator of "Billy Bunter."

Hume's discovery was inspired by billiards. For all we know the next clue to our future understanding of events may lie concealed in snooker!

The great attraction of billiard saloons[8] has been explained as follows:

- ✧ "Ye're oot the wey [out of the way], ye dinnie [don't] get into trouble, say fae [from] the auld crabs [old, sour people] that call the cops when ye're playin' fitba' [football] in the stree'."

- ✧ "The light's peaceful."

DARTS

These two varieties of darts perhaps are not very well known:

Killer

- ✧ "In this game ye've to throw the dart wi' the hand ye dinnie usually use. If ye hit say a number three, ye must hit a double three before ye 'come a killer. Ye have three lives and the idea is to kill everybody else that's playin'."

Chicken

- ✧ "That's a gey dangerous game! A laddie stands wi' the dart board above his heid. Darts are thrown and if he moves away, he's 'chicken'."

SHORE DIVERSIONS

The seashore provides both the setting and the material for many games:

- ✧ "Look for three tin cans and stick them on big rocks and fire stanes at them till ye knock them owre [over]."

- ✧ "Ye get a little bright stone or shell, and ye hide it in one o' three wee castles o' sand, and the person has to guess which."

---

[8] The artist Ben Nicholson is reported as saying of his student days: "And there was the billiard room . . . round the corner. The red ivory ball and the two whites, one with a spot and one without, and the clink of their relationships became an 'experience' far more related to art than anything they taught me at the Slade."

Here are three others:

Skiffers

❖ You select a flattish stone and fling it across the surface of the
water and see how many jumps you can make it do. You may
set yourself a number to aim at and play alone or you can
challenge others.

Cuddie, Come Quick!

❖ This is very popular (or used to be) at Seafield shore. A boy
stands in the middle of a group of boys and quickly throws a
half-brick up into the air, at the same time crying "Cuddie
[donkey], come quick!" The others round him try to hit that
brick with "yucks" or "yuckers [stones]" and in the same
instance the thrower has to get out the way. Mistakes are
frequent. The previous thrower-up of the half-brick decides
who throws next.

Tic Tac Tee

❖ This is a Musselburgh shore game. You take a red stone and
draw this diagram, like a kind of Union Jack, on a whiter,
flatter stone.

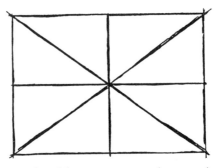

The game is played between two, and you each start off with
three men—three coloured stones or three shells—and the idea
is to get three of your men in a row either diagonally or along
the sides. The spaces (half-lines or half-diagonals) are called
"dullts" and as a matter of fact the person who gets the first
shot ought to win and if he's wise he places his first man in
the centre or "croun [crown]." After introducing each of your
three men in turn, you're allowed to shift a dullt at a time.
Sometimes the player who has one of his men on the croun

makes a mistake, which means he has to shift and so lose the game. At this point his opponent gleefully begins to sing (to the tune of the "Froth-Blower's Anthem"):

You'll have to move your crouner
Your crouner, your crouner:
You'll have to move your crouner
For it's Tic Tac Tee!

5

SINGLE AND DOUBLE BALLIE

A "Ballie" is a game played with a soft rubber ball, very often an old tennis ball. Sometimes more than one ball is used. You can play "Single Ballie," "Double Ballie," "Three Ballie," and even "Four Ballie." The ball is "stotted[1] [bounced]," usually against a wall or on the ground or off a ledge, and frequently it is thrown up into the air. And whenever it returns, either it's hit or thrown once more or else it's caught in the player's hands.

One of the simplest of these games is:

One Two Three A-Leerie

❖   One two three a-leerie
Four five six a-leerie
Seven eight nine a-leerie
Ten a-leerie, postman!

Open the gates and let me in, sir
Open the gates and let me in, sir
Open the gates and let me in, sir
Early in the morning!

As the rhyme starts the counting, you keep stotting the ball on the ground, and at the first "a-leerie" you lift your right leg over the ball; at the second "a-leerie," you lift your left leg

---

[1] James Ballantine, *Lament for Ancient Edinburgh* (1856):

The ancient [a]Krames whaur weanies [b]tottit	[b]*tottered*
Whaur a' wee [c]wairdless [d]callants trottit	[c]*spendrift* [d]*boys*
Though scantly fed, and [e]scrimply coatit	[e]*ill-clad*
To spend their a'	
On [f]dirlin' drums or [g]ba's that stottit	[f]*beating drums*
Against the [h]wa'.	[g]*balls* [h]*wall*

[a]*The Krames were the little street stalls in the narrow space between the Tolbooth and St Giles. They were open stalls in contrast to the Lucken [locked] booths.*

over; at the third, your right again; at the fourth, your left; and at "postman," after you stot the ball, you must "birl [turn]" right round and then catch it. In the second verse, every time you say "Open," you lift your leg over the ball, using your right and left legs turn about and at "Early in the morning" you birl as before.

"One Two Three A-Leerie" was a great favourite with the older generation. And so was this one:

One Two Three Four Five

❦ One two three four five
Can you catch a fish alive?
Why did you let it go?
Because it bit my finger so.

The girl picks up the hem of her skirt with her left hand, and with her other hand she starts stotting the ball on the ground. At "five," at "alive," at "go," and at "so," the ball has to bounce cleanly through the space between her arm and the picked-up skirt.

Ballie games that use the ground alone are rather out of favour nowadays. Stotting the ball against a wall is much more popular. One of the best is:

Plainie Clappie

❦ A Single Ballie with a variety of actions which the player chants. For each action the ball is thrown against the wall, and each must be correctly performed before the ball bounces back and is caught in the player's hands.

"Plainie": The ball is simply stotted against the wall.

"Clappie": Hands must be clapped.

"Rollie-pin [rolling-pin]": Hands are rolled over each other.

"To backie": Hands are clapped behind back.

"Right hand": Ball must be caught in right hand.

"Left hand": Ball must be caught in left hand.

"High si-toosh": Ball is caught with clasped hands, up-turned.

"Low si-toosh": Ball is caught with clasped hands, down-turned.

"Telephone": A hand is held up to the ear.

"The answer": A hand is held up to the mouth.

"Touch my heel": Hand must touch heel.

"Touch my toe": Hand must touch toe.

"Through ye go": Ball must go through legs.

"Big birly-O!": The player has to turn once around.

In "Plainie Clappie," the rhyme dictates the routine or pattern followed, and only one ball is used. But in Double Ballies, two balls are used:

Wallie

✧ A Double Ballie, in which a general pattern of eight actions is laid down:

1. Wallie: "Ye kick the wall."

2. Groundie: "Ye touch the ground wi' one hand."

3. Steeple: "One ball is thrown up in the air, and one against wall."

4. Bridge: "One ball is bounced plain, the other over hand."

5. Through ye go: "Ye put through your right leg."

6. Other leg: "Ye put through your left leg."

7. Bring it back: "Through your leg a different way."

8. Big birly-O!: "Ye turn around."

In each of these actions, the player has to deal with one ball after the other; and throughout she keeps on chanting a rhyme, or singing a song. A typical "Wallie chant" is:

Cinderella

✧ Cinderella
Dressed in yella
Went to the ball
To meet her fella.

And a typical song:

Away up in Holland

✧ Away up in Holland
The land of the Dutch
There lives a wee lassie
I love very much,

Her name is Susanna
But where is she now?
She's up in the mountains
A-milking the cow.

Incidentally, a "Double Ballie" is preferred to a "Single Ballie"—"Ye get a better rhythm."

Sixers

✧ Another popular routine, in which the ball is bounced against the wall in six different ways:

    1. In a plain way.
    2. Under right leg.
    3. Under left leg.
    4. Through open legs from front.
    5. Through open legs from back.
    6. From behind back.

In "Plain Sixers" you don't use a chant or a song. You simply follow the plan doing every action once, follow this by doing each twice, and so on up to six times. After that you go down the scale. But in most "Sixers" chants or songs are employed. A song like:

Rabbie Burns

✧ Rabbie Burns was born in Ayr
Now he's in Trafalgar Square:
If ye want to see him there
Jump on a bus and skip the fare!

Or a chant:

Fudge, Fudge

✧ Fudge, fudge
Tell the judge
My mother's had a baby:

Joy, joy
It's a boy
It's driving my mother crazy.

"Sixers can be played either as a 'Single Ballie' or as a 'Double Ballie'."

One of the lengthiest patterns is "Plainie Dummie [dumb] Stookie [stucco]," which also requires a rhyme to be chanted or sung throughout:

✧ "If I was doing a double ballie 'Plainie Dummie Stookie,' I'd start wi' 'O X O,' because that's the simplest thing to say while ye're concentrating on playing."

Here is the whole protracted ritual:

Plainie Dummie Stookie

✧ Plainie: "Ye stot [bounce] the ball against the wall."
Dummie: "Ye're silent."
Stookie: "Ye keep your legs stiff and straight."
Dummie-Stookie: "Ye dae [do] baith [both]."
Runnie: "Ye run on the spot."
Jumpie: "Ye jump up and doun."
Hoppie: "Left foot."
Hoppie: "Right foot."
Two legs: "Side hop with alternate legs."
Wee man: "Ye go doun."
Medium man: "Half up."
Tall man: "On your toes."
Heelie: "Stand on heels."
Toe-ie: "Stand on toes."
Walkie: "Ye walk."
Marchie: "Ye march."

Having successfully performed this "Plainie," you go right through the ritual "Dummie" ("saying the rhyme in to your-sel'"), then "Stookie" and so on to "Marchie." Some players do "Blindie" as well—that's with your eyes shut all the time. As can be imagined, the full game can last a very long time: "Playing it in the playground efter we got oot, we were that late gettin' hame wir [our] mothers wondered where we were." Clearly it has "the fascination of what's difficult." And this is one of the many rhymes that can be chosen:

Ashes to Ashes

✧ Ashes to ashes
Dust to dust:
Come on now honey
Ye must, ye must!

We also have a number of single and double ballies where actions are carried through more or less matching the words of the rhymes used—on the same lines as "Plainie Clappie":

Charlie Chaplin

✧ Charlie Chaplin went to France
To show the ladies how to dance
First your heel and then your toe
Lift your skirts and through we go!

These rhymes follow their own special pattern and include such examples as "Oxo Cubes are Good for You," "Oliver Twist you Can't do This," "I Love to Birl Around," and "When I was One, I Ate a Bun." Another is the old skipping-chant "Are You Going to Golf, Sir?":

Are You Going to Golf, Sir.

✧ "Are you going to golf, sir?"
"No, sir." "Why, sir?"
"Because I've got a cold, sir."
"Where did you get the cold, sir?"
"Up at the North Pole, sir."
"What were you doing there, sir?"
"Catching polar bears, sir."
"How many did you catch, sir?"
"One, sir, two, sir,
Three, sir, four, sir,
Five, sir, six, sir,
Seven, sir, eight, sir,
Nine, sir, ten, sir,
That's all I got, sir!"

This follows the same sort of routine as "Wallie" and "Sixers," except that each time the word "sir" is said, the ball must be stotted on the ground.

When a good many girls all want to play Double Ballie, one game for which a cry may go up, is:

Matthew Mark Luke & John

⋄ A follow-my-leader game, in which the players queue up behind each other. The first one bounces each of the two balls, saying:

> Matthew Mark Luke and John:
> Next person carry on!

As the balls bounce back, the next person catches them, and then she repeats the same rhyme and the same business. Any one who fails stands out, and the last player left in wins.

There's also a Single Ballie for several players:

Ledgie

⋄ "Ye bounce the ball off a ledge on a wall, and each time ye catch it ye count by five, ten, fifteen, twenty, up to a hundred. Then ye move back a pace, and ye keep on doing that till ye're oot. The one that gets the farthest back from the wall wins."

And here's another ballie game which, however, is rather different from those which have already been described:

Jumping Over the Moon

⋄ "So many of youse stand in a long line, and if you're at the front, ye fling the ba' up against the wa' and as it stots back ye jump owre it (letting it go between your legs) and the person behind ye catches it and they do what you done and the next person catches the ba' and so on. As you jump over the ball ye say a name beginning with *A* and so does everybody else. The next round it'll be *B* and ye go right through the alphabet. You can also say the name of a tree or a flower, or if ye're stuck for thae [those] kind o' names, ye can choose anything ye see roond about ye, like 'curtain' or 'windie [window]' or 'lamp-post.' If ye dinnie jump owre [over] the moon right, cannie [can't] say a name, or let the ba' fa', ye have to sit oot, and the last yin left in wins the game."

These are some of the rhymes used for "Wallie" and "Sixers":

Chinga-linga-Chinaman

❖ Chinga-linga-Chinaman
Had a toffee shop
He sold ginger
Lemonade and pop,

All his customers
Used to call him Chop
Chinga-linga-Chinaman
Closed his shop.

Charlie Chaplin

❖ Charlie Chaplin
Washed up
Broke a saucer
And *C U P*
Spells cup.

Dopey Dinah

❖ Dopey Dinah went to China
In a plate of semolina.

Instead of "plate" you often hear "box." And the couplet comes into this other game:

"This is what we dae. Ye've got to get a good slidey wa' and ye a' stand wi' your backs to it, and ye keep on sayin' the rhyme and ye sway fae [from] side to side athoot [without] movin' your feet."

Gain, Gain

❖ Gain, gain
*a*Ba', ba'   *a ball*
Twenty lassies in a *b*raw   *b row*
No a laddie amang them a'
Gain, gain
Ba', ba'.

Jean and John

❖ Jean and John
Up a tree
K I S S
I N G,

G

First comes love
Then comes marriage
Then comes John
With the baby's carriage.

Has any other poet ever put over his meaning so skilfully—by
spelling out instead of speaking a word—and at the same time
rhyming on one of the spelt-out letters? Only this anonymous
one—or many!

Mother Says

✧ Mother says I musn't
Mother says I musn't
No sir, thank you, not just yet;

If you give me time
If you give me time
I'll think it over, maybe you'll be mine.

Mother, Mother, I am Ill

✧ "Mother, mother I am ill
Send for the doctor up the hill."
"Up the hill is far too far."
"Then we'll buy a motor car."
"A motor car is far too dear."
"Then we'll buy a pint of beer."
"A pint of beer is far too strong."
"Then we'll buy a treacle scone."
"A treacle scone is far too tough."
"Then we'll buy a box of snuff."
"A box of snuff will make you sneeze."
"Then we'll buy a pound of cheese."
"A pound of cheese will make you sick."
"So send for the doctor, quick, quick, quick!"

Also for skipping.

Mrs Blue

✧ Mrs Blue
Lost her shoe
In the morning
She had flu.

Mrs Mackay

Mrs Mackay
Has a stye in her eye:
The doctor says
She'll have to die.

Mrs Magee

Mrs Magee
She went to tea
Shut the door
And turned the key.

Mrs Murray

Mrs Murray
Was in a hurry
To catch a train
To *a*Musselburry.   *a Musselburgh*

Mrs Wright

Mrs Wright
Got a fright
In the middle
Of the night.

She saw a ghost
Eating toast
Half-way up
The lamp-post.

The Abbeyhill Miner

My wee man's a miner
He lives in Abbeyhill:
He gets his *a*pey on *b*Setterday   *a pay*   *b Saturday*
And buys a half a gill.

He goes to church on Sunday
Half an *c*hour late: *c* pron. *oor*
He *d*pu's the buttons off his shirt   *d pulls*
And *e*pits them in the plate.   *e puts*

Oh Mother, Mother

Oh mother, mother what a cold I've got
Drinking tea and coffee hot:

Wrap me up in a nice big shawl
And take me to the doctor.

Doctor, doctor, shall I die?
No, my darling, you shan't die:
Take this medicine twice a day
And that will cure your cold away!

Also used for skipping.

One Two Three Gibraltar

One two three Gibraltar
My husband's name is Walter:
If you think it necessary
Look it up in the dictionary.

or: ### One Two Three A-larry

One two three a-larry
My husband's name is Larry . . .

One Two Three A-wallie

One two three a-wallie
Four five six a-wallie
Seven eight nine a-wallie
Ten a-wallie, alla-hoy!

The next verse is "a-groundie," the next "a-stampie," and so on.

Over the Garden Wa'

Over the garden ^awa'   ^a *wall*
I let the baby ^bfa':   ^b *fall*
My mother came out
And ^cskelped my ^ddowp   ^c *smacked* ^d *bottom*
Over the garden wa'.

Popeye the Sailorman

Popeye the Sailorman
Lives in a caravan
He likes to go swimmin'
To see all the women
Popeye the Sailorman.

Here are some of the rhymes used for "Plainie Dummie Stookie":

Boy, Girl

❖ Boy, girl
Garden gate
Stand talking
Very late:

Father comes
Big boots
Boy runs
Girl scoots.

Dark Tan

❖ Dark tan
Light tan
Every colour
But tartan.

Eachy Peachy

❖ Eachy peachy pelly plum
Throw the ᵃtatties up the ᵇlum!   *ᵃ potatoes ᵇ chimney*

Jack be Nimble

❖ Jack be nimble
Jack be quick
Jack jump over
The candle-stick
Stick, stick
And over the stick.

Jenny Wren

❖ Jenny Wren
Stole a hen
Never let her
Mammie ᵃken.   *ᵃ know*

Lemonade and Water

❖ Lemonade and water
Is good for my wee daughter.

Nigger Nigger

❖ Nigger, nigger
Pull the trigger
Bang! bang! bang!

Tiddly Tiddly Barber

✧ ^aTiddly tiddly barber   *^a drunken*
   Went to shave his father:
   The razor slipped
   And cut his lip
   Tiddly tiddly barber.

Wee Shirley Temple

✧ Wee Shirley Temple
   Bought a penny doll:
   She washed it, she dressed it
   Then she let it fall.

   She phoned for the doctor
   The doctor couldn't come:
   She phoned for the ambulance
   Tong! tong! tong!

Also used for skipping.

The Nice Meringue

✧ Would you like this nice meringue,
   Am I ^aricht or am I ^bwrang?   *^a right ^b wrong*

And, lastly, here are a few other Double Ballie rhymes:

Oxo Cubes

✧ Oxo cubes are good for you
   This is the way you put them through:
   First the right and then the left—
   Don't bend down or you'll burst your vest.

Oliver Twist

✧ Oliver Twist
   You can't do this
   So what's the use of trying O?
   If so
   Do so
   Touch your toe
   Through you go
   Big birly-O!

I Love to Birl

✧   I love to *a*birl around   *a turn*
    To touch the ground
    To show my shoe
    To put it through
    To draw it back
    To flipperty-flap.

To "flipperty-flap" means to clap your hands first in front of you and then behind your back—before catching the bouncing ball.

Wake up Johnnie

✧   Wake up, Johnnie, light the fire
    Turn the gas a wee bit higher,
    Go and call the Black Maria
    Jeannie's got the toothache.

This goes to the same tune as *In and Out the Dusting Bluebells* and besides being a Double Ballie rhyme, it's often sung in another game:

✧   "Ye have a ball inside a nylon stocking and ye bang it against the wa', up and down, then across-ways, and then under the legs."

Perhaps the most popular of all Double Ballies is:

Gipsy Gipsy

✧   Also called "Ipsy Gipsy." The actions required in this game are stated at the side of each verse. The two balls are bounced against a wall in every verse except the second last when they are thrown up into the air. The actions must be performed in the time between throwing the balls and catching them. And they have to be caught at each key word—which is in italics.

        Gipsy Gipsy lived in a *tent*   ["*You stot the ball plain.*"
        Couldn't afford to pay for a *tent*:
        When the *tent* man came next day
        Gipsy Gipsy *tented* away.

        Gipsy Gipsy lived in a *stable*   ["*You curtsey.*"
        Couldn't afford to pay for a *stable*:
        When the *stable* man came next day
        Gipsy Gipsy *stabled* away.

Gipsy Gipsy lived in a *boom*   ["*You crouch down.*"
Couldn't afford to pay for a *boom*:
When the *boom* man came next day
Gipsy Gipsy *boomed* away.

Gipsy Gipsy lived in a *bob*   ["*You bob up.*"
Couldn't afford to pay for a *bob*:
When the *bob* man came next day
Gipsy Gipsy *bobbed* away.

Gipsy Gipsy lived in a *stamp*   ["*You stamp your foot.*"
Couldn't afford to pay for a *stamp*:
When the *stamp* man came next day
Gipsy Gipsy *stamped* away.

Gipsy Gipsy lived in a *steeple*   ["*You throw the balls*
Couldn't afford to pay for a *steeple*:   *up in the air.*"
When the *steeple* man came next day
Gipsy Gipsy *steepled* away.

Gipsy Gipsy lived in a *dover*   ["*You throw the*
Couldn't afford to pay for a *dover*:   *balls overhand or*
When the *dover* man came next day   *over-shoulder.*"
Gipsy Gipsy *dovered* away.

Gipsy Gipsy lived in a *tent stable boom bob*   ["*You do the*
    stamp steeple dover   *lot!*"
Couldn't afford to pay for the *tent stable boom bob stamp*
    steeple dover
When the *tent stable boom bob stamp steeple dover* man came
next day
Gipsy Gipsy *tented stabled boomed bobbed stamped steepled*
    dovered away!

Finally, here is a long Ballie Song which calls for illustration of the second line in each verse:

When I Was One

    When I was one
    I ate a bun
    Going out to sea
    I jumped aboard a Chinaman's ship
    And the Chinaman said to me:
    "O this way, that way, forward, backway, *A B C.*"

When I was two
I buckled my shoe. . . .

When I was three
I climbed a tree . . .

When I was four
I kicked the door. . . .

When I was five
I pushed over a hive. . . .

When I was six
I chopped up sticks. . . .

When I was seven
I went to Devon. . . .

When I was eight
I jumped the gate. . . .

When I was nine
I hurt my spine. . . .

When I was ten
I wrote with a pen. . . .

There are numerous variations of the number verses and even of the chorus—such as:

Uppie, uppie
Like a puppie
A B C. . . .

6

PEEVERS

During the last thirty or forty years this game appears to have evolved newer and more varied forms of play. Peevers [hopscotch]—also called "Peeverie Beds," or "Peeveries," or "Beds"—may be described as a hopping-game requiring a pattern of chalked beds or boxes over which the "peever" is pushed by a hopping foot—according to agreed rules. The "peever"[1] is usually an empty round tin box (very often an old boot-polish tin), or it may be a piece of tile. A favourite material at one time was marble—which was coaxed from the nearest monumental mason's. Occasionally the peever was made of slate. Or it might be an old bung from a barrel. Long ago the glassworks turned out glass peevers—there's an example made of Holyrood glass, in the Huntly House Museum. The boxes or beds for peevers are chalked on the pavements, and very often the asphalt in certain streets provides an ideal surface for playing on. In some parts of peevers the player walks instead of hopping, and sometimes the peever is carried. Girls love drawing out the beds, their numbering carries a personal touch especially the figure one, which is laced with loops and finely placed. An Edinburgh street wouldn't look the same without this gay and lively geometry.

Plain Beds

Plain Beds

✧ In "Plain Beds" (or "Boxie") the boxes are arranged and numbered as follows:

"We usually do the numbers double so that you can make them out better. It goes for the chalk though! We maybe manage single and finish double wi' a stane that writes."

[1] Fr. *pierre*.

Plain Beds or Boxie

The beds may contain six, nine, twelve, or any number of boxes. "R" means you can rest with both feet in that box, "H" means you have to hop. The peever-players can mark any box a resting-box or a hopping-box, just as they think fit.

"You can make it *all* rests, but we like it wi' no rests, for it's harder, ye have more fun."

"Most people play 'hoppie-restie' or 'hoppie-layie'—that is, you hop in one bed and rest in the next. Even numbers 'hoppie,' odd numbers 'restie'."

"To start the game, you either agree the order, or some lassie shouts 'Who wants to be first?' and the first person to say 'First' gets first, and the 'Second' gets second, and so on: but of course that lassie that shouts usually says 'Who wants to be first? First!' and so *she's* first."

The rules for this summer game are very simple. The player has to hop on one and the same foot. After being pushed, the peever must land in the box aimed-for without ending up on a line or touching a line. The player's hopping foot mustn't touch a line, and, when resting, neither foot must touch a line. By "kicking" the peever is meant (usually) giving it a stab or sharp push with the hopping foot. By a "jump" is very often meant a hopping jump. A beginner at peevers is termed a "black sheep," a skilled player a "black jack."

In plain beds there are fourteen rounds to be accomplished:

1. *Oneie, Twoie, Threeie, Fourie, Fiveie, Sixie.* You start from 1 and the peever is pushed by the hopping player from box to box finishing in 6 and pushing back to 1. Then from 1 it is skiffed by hand or kicked with the foot into 2, pushed as before to 6 and back to 1. After that it is skiffed to 3, 4, 5, 6, and so on. This performance is repeated starting from 6 and going back to 1.

2. *Spell your Name.* Using only the two boxes 1 and 6 you hop from 1 to 6 and back again, spelling out the letters of your name. Then you kick the peever into 6, and back into 1, and now while hopping you push it into 6, leaving it there while you hop all round the beds back to 6. Then you push into 5 and repeat what you've done and so on for all the numbers.

3. *Sixie-Sixie.* Push the peever into 2 while hopping then into 6, then into 1. (Twoie-Sixie).
Push the peever into 3, jump into 3, push it while hopping into 6, then back to 1 (Threeie-Sixie).
Then you do Fourie-Sixie, Fiveie-Sixie and Sixie-Sixie.

4. *Hop Round the World.* Push the peever into 2 and hop all the way round to 1. Push peever into 3 and hop all the way round to 1. And so on.

5. *Half-Lineie.* Stamp one foot on line between 1 and 2, then bend down and push peever into 3 and jump on to next line and so on.

6. *Whole Lineie.* You push peever into 2, jump with both feet on first line between 1 and 2, push peever into 3 and jump on to next line and so on.

7. *Punch and Judy.* The peever is pushed into 2, then you jump so that your legs straddle 1 and 5, then 2 and 6. The peever is next pushed to 3 and your legs straddle 3 and 5, then

2 and 4. This performance is repeated to the words "Dance dolly dance!"

8. *Cheesie.* The peever is hidden somewhere in the beds and you have to hop and rest your way round, looking neither up nor down but perfectly straightforward and if you touch the peever you're out.

9. *Blindie.* You hide your eyes while the other players place the peever somewhere on the beds. Then you have to walk right round the beds without stepping on a line and without standing on the peever. As you go round the boxes, "Butter!" is shouted when you step clear, and "Cheese!" when you stand on a line. "Blindie" is done both forwards and backwards.

10. *High Sky or Skyie.* The same ritual as "blindie," only you walk with your head looking upwards.

Mixed Beds

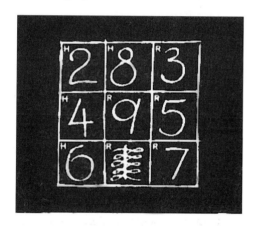

11. *Headie.* You have to negotiate the round of the boxes with the peever on your head.

12. *Handie.* You have to negotiate the round of the boxes with the peever on your hand.

13. *Shoulderie.* You have to negotiate the round of the boxes with the peever on your shoulder.

14. *Footie.* You have to negotiate the round of the boxes with the peever on your foot.

After you have performed this whole series of "rituals" successfully you're allowed to pick any box and chalk your name on it. When all the boxes are filled with names the player with the biggest number of boxes is the winner. If you fail at any point in the game you give way to the next player but when your turn comes round again you start from the stage you left off.

MIXED BEDS

Mixed Beds

✧ This is played exactly the same as plain beds and has the same arrangement of boxes, only they are numbered differently.
The resting and hopping beds are so spaced out that the player has a double box to jump. Some even like to jump three boxes.

"It's harder and the game lasts longer."

OXO BEDS

Oxo Beds

✧ In "Oxo Beds," "Sixie-Sixie," or "Sidie Beds," you play exactly the same as in plain beds, only you don't play in or out the "oxo" or "sixie-sixie" box. It doesn't come into use until the end, when the player does another first round. When she comes to Sixie, she kicks the peever into this box, hops in, kicks it out across the north line, and says "O," hops out, kicks it back, hops back, kicks it out across the east line and says "X," hops out, kicks it back, hops back, kicks it out across the south line and says "O," hops out, kicks it back and shouts "Oxo!" That's the end.

"Sixie-Sixie" is played the very same, except that you say "sixie" and at the finish the player shouts "sixie-sixie!"

Oxo Beds

Sixie–Sixie

LETTER BEDS

Letter Beds

❖ "You choose any letter of the alphabet and draw it big so that you can make about ten boxes in it."

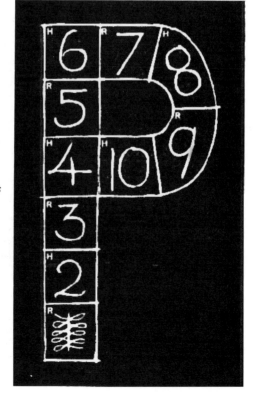

Letter Beds

A Variety of Beds

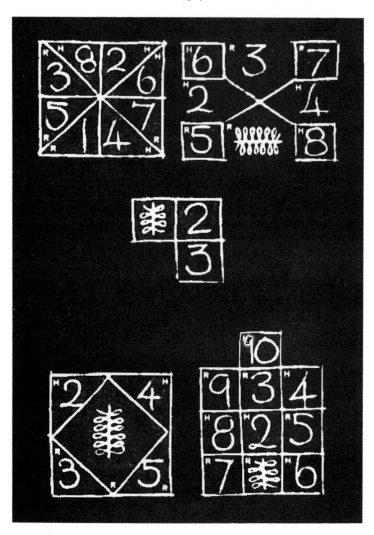

Eightie Beds   Crossie Beds

Threeie Beds

Fiveie Beds   Tenie Beds

"You put the tin [peever] into 'oneie' and you kick it into 'twoie,' then into 'threeie,' 'fourie' . . . right up to 'tenie.' And when you've done that, you can mark your initials in any box you like, and after that somebody else gets a shot. In going round the beds they have to hop over your box, but when your turn comes round you can rest in your box. When all the boxes have been filled up with initials, the player that has the most boxes wins the game."

Using a letter bed you can almost do the whole game of plain beds.

A VARIETY OF BEDS

The game of peevers as outlined in plain beds can be played in various beds, where new arrangements of boxes have been developed such as "Crossie Beds," "Eightie Beds," "Threeie Beds," "Fiveie Beds," and "Tenie Beds."

❖ "Why we play 'Crossie Beds' is just for the decoration in the middle."

Twenty Beds
or
Starry Beds

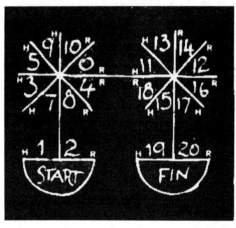

TWENTY BEDS, OR STARRY BEDS

Twenty Beds

❖ Using these linked, double-star beds, the ordinary game of peevers is more or less played—as in plain beds. Nearly all the rounds are done backwards as well as forwards except the last which is "blindie."

H

Aeroplane Beds

Aeroplane Beds

❖ After plain beds, this is the most popular form of peevers. These aeroplane-shaped beds first began to appear in the late 1920s, just as aviation was coming more and more to the fore. In place of "London" we sometimes find a boy's name, such as "Tom Brown."

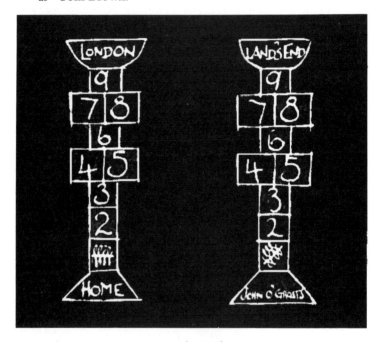

Aeroplane Beds

"Home," "London," and boxes 4, 5, 7, and 8 are all resting beds. In the first round, when the peever is kicked or skiffed into 7, 8, 9, or London, you can get "keppies [catches]," if it's agreed. To prevent the peever over-running, another player stands with her feet together—like the boys do in bools. You're also allowed "rollies" and "bumps," if it's agreed. That means you can take the shot over again if the peever rolls out of a box or if bumpy ground hinders its passage.

1. *Up and Down the Scale.* You start from "home," skiff or kick the peever into 1, jump [hop] into 2, into 3, rest your left

leg in 4, your right leg in 5, give a jumping hop into 6, do 7 and 8, hop back, doing the boxes just as before until you get to 2. As you stand hopping in there, you bend down, pick the peever out of 1 (with your hand), then hop into 1 and hop "home." Next you skiff or kick the peever into 2, hop into 1, jump [hop] over 2, and into 3 and from there you carry on hopping to London, turn and come back in the usual way until you get to 3 where you pick the peever out of 2, and then hop "home." Play proceeds in this manner until the peever is skiffed into "London." You hop up to 9, then hop out of this box and go hopping round the outside of "London" and there you pick up the peever and then jump into "London," lay down the peever, hop "home" and return to "London." From "London" the peever is skiffed to 9, you jump over it, hop "home" and come back to 8, pick up the peever from 9, hop into 9 and then into "London." The peever is next skiffed into 8 and you continue "down the scale" until you have "worked your way home."

2. *Hoppy All the Way.* You push or kick the peever in the usual fashion to London and back home again without taking a single rest.

3. *Restie All the Way.* You work the peever to London and back home again resting in every box.

4. *Blindie.* You shut your eyes or you're blindfolded and you've to walk to "London" and come back "home." You mustn't step on the peever which is placed somewhere in the beds and you mustn't tread on a line. If you don't the cry is "Butter!" or "Margarine!" If you do, it's "Cheese!" or "Cheddar!" If your walk's successful, you get to pick a box and put your name on it. In further "blindies," while you can stand in that box, every other player has to jump over it. The player who can claim the most boxes wins the game.

Some players add rounds of "handie," "footie," "shoulderie" "headie," "high sky," and "cheesie"—as in plain beds. The fact is nearly every street has its own special version of aeroplane beds.

ROUNDIE BEDS, OR CIRCLE BEDS

Roundie Beds

✧ In "Roundie Beds," or "Circle Beds," the circles chalked are about two feet or so in diameter and up to twenty in number. You hop and pick the peever from "start" to "end" and back again and after performing this feat you're allowed to choose a bed in which you write your name and on which you can rest during future hops. No one else can do so, the other players have to jump over your box or boxes. The winner is the one who can claim the most boxes.

Roundie Beds can be arranged in zig-zags, big circles or in any pattern that the players like to devise.

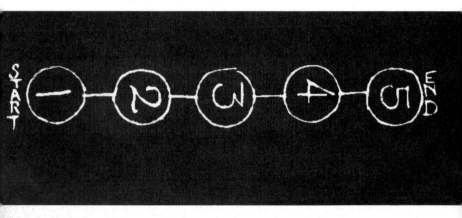

Roundie Beds

INVISIBLE BEDS

Invisible Beds

✧ "When ye've nae chalk ye just yase [use] the squarie shapes o' the pavement, and ye ca' that 'Invisible Beds.'"

HOPPIE BEDS, OR HOPPIE ALL THE WAY

In 'Hoppie Beds," or "Hoppie All the Way," no peever is used. There are plenty of such "hoppie" games, and for them many picturesque beds have been thought out.

Banana Skins

✧ Ten banana-curved lines about five inches apart are chalked on the street or pavement. They are numbered from one up to ten. The player has to hop from one to ten and then back to one again. No rests are allowed. The hopping is done on one foot—sideways—if you stand on a line you're out. If you do a successful hop, "you get a banana," which signifies that you can write your name on any line you choose, and after that, when hopping, you may "rest on your own banana." On the other hand, you must hop over any banana or bananas belonging to other players. The hopper who collects the biggest bunch of bananas wins.

Linie Beds

✧ This is exactly similar to banana skins, except that you hop between "straight bananas."

"We dinnie [don't] number the lines. We write the lassies' names, one along each line, but no their real names, their names mixed-up, like instead o' Jean Wright and Valerie Tait we'd write Jean Tait and Valerie Wright, and if Doreen Shuffle-botham hopped all the way and picked Jean Tait's line, she'd first put down a cross in the space and then scribble her ain [own] name."

Linie Beds

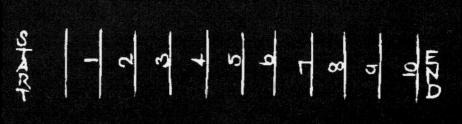

Roundie Beds

❖ "Roundie Beds," or "Circle Beds," can also be used for a hoppie.

Squarie Beds

❖ You can have any number of boxes up to twenty, if you like. A successful hop means you can choose a square, initial it, and after that, though *you* can rest there, every other hopper must avoid it, and this necessitates a longer hopping jump. The idea is to win as many squares as possible.

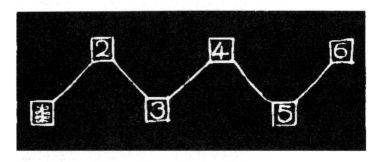

Squarie Beds

T.B. Beds

❖ As in the other hoppie games you try to get your name in as many spaces as possible, where you can rest, but over which the other hoppers have to jump. But, both approaching London and on the turn round, every one is allowed to rest in the T.B. bed, one foot in the T, and one in the B.

Snailie

❖ This is a "hoppie all the way" of the same sort of style, only the figure is a spiral crossed out in boxes and following the pattern of a great ram's-horn shell. The snailie beds can also be used for a peever game.

BALLIE PEEVERS

Ballie Peevers

❖ "Ye jist use plain beds and a ba' instead o' a peever. You roll the ball into oneie, hop efter [after] it, stop it and stot [bounce] it,

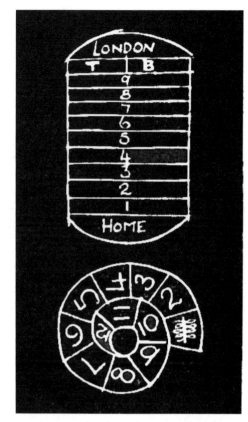

T.B. Beds

Snailie Beds

then roll it into twoie, hop efter it, stop it and stot it in twoie, and ye keep on doing like that till ye get to sixie, and after sixie, ye go back the wey [way] and if ye do a' that, ye get to pick a bed for yoursel', and the one wi' the maist [most] beds wins. You do the same rules as in or'nary peevers and ye must stot the ba' right."

In conclusion

How is it that girls are so devoted to this natural geometry? As far as they're concerned the subject is usually written off. And very often the young, hopping Euclids are banned from the schools:

❖ "In ma last school ye got the belt for drawin' peever beds in the playground. Fae the heidmaister tae!"

- "In oor school ye were allowed to play beds so long as it was ootside the gates."

- "At Abbeyhill ye could play peevers in the playground but the jannie [janitor] was aye moanin'."

In a sense every ring-game is a tribute to the circle, from centre to circumference while in peevers the lassies do homage to the square, on all its sides and also diagonally. A ring-game presents an opera—with dancing. Peevers is a ballet—without music. It has curious "swift, slow" graces. And so have the other hopping games, especially when chance demands dainty stepping directly after tremendous leaping. If birds besides flying went in for dancing, you'd see something very like hopscotch!

7

SKIPPING

Most Edinburgh girls learn to skip at an early age—from about three—and skipping continues all through their school-days, but after leaving school at fifteen their jumping-ropes are cast aside.

Skipping-Games

Simple skipping hardly needs describing, but the full art[1] that almost every girl acquires is rather intricate. A youngster sent the "messages [errands]" often takes her jumping-ropes with her. She has a big choice of songs or chants that she can skip to and even when she is by herself she usually sings or says them aloud. Here is one that combines skipping with hopping:

Down to the Baker's Shop
✧ Down to the baker's shop
Hop hop hop!
For my mother said
Buy a loaf of bread,
Down to the baker's shop
Hop hop hop!

Skipping on one foot alone is called "Hoppie" or "Hoppie on one leg." Young skippers practise a lot by themselves, for they must be able to skip backwards as well as forwards, and in "Crossie"[2] the hands have to be crossed over. To allow the

[1] In *Notes on the Movements of Young Children* (1874), R. L. S. has described a "mistress of the art of skipping." Not in Edinburgh but "in the familiar neighbourhood of Hampstead . . . There were two sisters from seven to nine perhaps. . . . The elder . . . was just and adroit in every movement; the rope passed over her black head and under her scarlet-stockinged legs with a precision and regularity that was like machinery; but there was nothing mechanical. . . ."

[2] "There was one variation favourite with her, in which she crossed her hands before her with a motion not unlike weaving. . . ." *Notes on the Movements of Young Children* (1874).

whirling rope to pass, the skipper must have both feet lifted in the air, and afterwards while some may let both feet together touch the ground, a number of players prefer the style of hitting the ground again with either foot alternately. Sometimes in the street you may see a girl skipping her solitary self, but gradually her chums begin to gather round. She's then very likely to come out with one of the oldest skipping verses:

I Call in my Very Best Friend
⌁   I call in my very best friend
    And that is Lynda Phillips:
    One, two, three!

Lynda then jumps in, and the pair of them carry on skipping, perhaps to the singing of:

Whistle While you Work
⌁   Whistle while you work!
    Jenny made a shirt:
    Jessie wore it, Benny tore it
    Mary made it worse!

At this stage Lynda jumps out, and another "best friend" is given an invitation to jump in. A single skipper may also make a game of inviting more than one. She rarely copes with more than two, usually one at the back and one at the front. Then they sing out:

⌁   How many *ª*messages can you carry?   *ª goods bought*
    One, two, three, four, five, six . . .

And they find out what number they can skip to—without tripping over or catching the rope. During the springtime months girls who are chums frequently skip to and from school. The two of them move at a fair pace each of them in turn skipping in or out of a rope which never stops "birling [turning]" round.[3]

3 "And when the two took the rope together and whirled in and out!..." *Notes on the Movements of Young Children* (1874).

✦ I wish *ᵃthe night was Saturday night   ᵃ *tonight*
     Tomorrow will be Sunday:
     I'll be dressed in all my best
     To go out with my Johnnie. . . .

But although one can skip alone and two skippers can get good fun together, the game of skipping is essentially a sociable one, so that if many want to play, then the more the merrier.

All in Together

✦ All in together
     Frosty weather:
     One, two, three!

     All out together
     Frosty weather:
     One, two, three!

The skippers jump in and then out again at "one," "two," and "three." In such a game two girls are engaged in "ca'ing [turning]" the rope for the others. But as soon as one of the skippers trips or stops the turning-rope she has to "take an end" or "take her end"—in other words, replace one of the "ca'ers [turners]." In skipping, as in peevers and many other games, a beginner or young child is known as a "black sheep." A black sheep can never be out or made to "ca' " the rope. So in this way newcomers or youngsters get a fair chance of picking up this traditional art. Those who are adepts are distinguished as "white sheep."

✦ "There are different weys [ways] o' startin' a game o' skippin'. Ye could play tatties [potatoes, a counting-out rhyme] to see who's to take their end. The last two people left in are on their ends. Or else, at the beginnin', somebody shouts 'Nae [no] end!' and the last two people to say 'Nae end!' take their end. And o' thae [those] two that's to hold the rope, yin [one] o' them is bound to cry 'First end!' meanin' that she'll go off her end first when the first person trips."

✦ "Another thing that often happens when ye start is this. Some lassie is sure to cry 'Ha'pennies!' or 'Nae [no] ha'pennies!' and 'Ha'pennies' means that if somebody trips and has to take their end, the lassie that comes oot [out], she can start jumpin' right

away, but 'Nae ha'pennies!' means she has to take her place at
the end o' the line.'

This last rule remains in force only for one game. These cries
are generally raised during a game whenever some one trips.
The player who joins the skippers usually calls "Ha'pennies"
or somebody calls it for her. But the girls making up the line
are more likely to get in first with "Nae ha'pennies!" The best
skipper seldom needs to take her end, she's always first in the
line of players and as long she's first she picks the games that
are to be played.

The "follow-my-leader" is by far the favourite style in
nearly all skipping games, since this allows everyone to take
part. One of the happiest is "Keep the Pot Boiling" or "Keep
the Kettle Boiling," each girl jumping in to say her bit:

Keep the Pot Boiling

  ⋄ Keep the pot boiling for Mrs Coleman's [a]claes !   [a] *clothes*
     Keep the kettle boiling for Mrs Adam's tea!

Or the choice very often falls on:

Grannie in the Kitchen

  ⋄ Grannie in the kitchen
     Doin' some stitchin'
     In comes the bogey man
     And chases grannie [a]oot!   [a]*out*

As one girl (the bogey man) jumps in, the skipper (grannie)
jumps out. But in most of the skipping games some sort of
action has to be performed by the girl who is skipping.

  ⋄ Teddy-bear, Teddy-bear, twirl around
     Teddy-bear, Teddy-bear, touch the ground
     Teddy-bear, Teddy-bear, show your shoe
     Teddy-bear, Teddy-bear, that will do. . . .

Sometimes two girls are brought in, one at "Kings" and one
at "Queens."

  ⋄ Kings and Queens
     And partners two

All dressed up in
Royal blue.

Stand at ease
Bend your knees
Salute to the east
And bow to the west. . . .

There appears to be no pattern of human behaviour that's been left out of this world of the turning rope from shaking hands ("How do You Do?") to goose-stepping ("At the Battle of Waterloo") and including, naturally, dancing of every description.

The Monster of Loch Ness
 ❖ I'm the Monster of Loch Ness
My name you'll never guess,
I can wave like a snake
And do the hippy shake,
I'm the Monster of Loch Ness!

Besides the general kind of follow-my-leader there's also one or two special types. "One No Miss" means that the skipper has to do one jump for every line that's chanted, "Two No Miss" two jumps, and "Four No Miss" four jumps. The months of the year are greatly used for this, being chanted singly for "One No Miss," in pairs for "Two No Miss" and for "Four No Miss" arranged like this:

January, February
 ❖ January, February, March, April
May, June, July, August
September, October, November, December.

"Ten and a Journey" is another follow-my-leader, in which the first skipper skips for ten jumps, then a rhyme begins, she jumps out, goes a journey round the green or playground, all the others doing exactly the same and following her back to the ropes again.

So far only "plain ropes," or "plain skipping," has been touched on. It is often called "beat skipping," since the rope turns to the usual beat or at the normal pace. Some skipping-games start off with the rope gently swaying to and fro—"wavie." The skipper jumps up and down to let the wavie rope pass back and forward, and then a little later (at "o-over") the rope makes a complete turn and continues to do so for the rest of the rhyme:

> *Bluebells & Cockle-Shells*
>
> ✧   Bluebells and cockle shells
> Eevie, ivy, o-over!
> Dr Brown is a very good man
> He teaches children all he can:
> First to read and then to write,
> Eevie, ivy, I pop out!

Many games begin with this swaying rope, among them "Christopher Columbie-a" and (turning full circle at "Cockie leekie"):

> *Edinburgh, Leith*
>
> ✧   Edinburgh, Leith,
> Portobello, Musselburgh
> And Dalkeith;
>
> Cockie leekie
> Hennie deekie
> One, two, three!

In "Baby in the Cradle" the rope is held high and whipped in a smaller circle above the kneeling player before being turned in a bigger circle for skipping. Stopping the rope is also an important feature of some games:

> *I Had a Little Dolly*
>
> ✧   I had a little dolly
> And its name was Sis,
> I took her to a Ball
> And she stopped like this.

At "this" the skipper has to catch the rope between her legs; and in "I'm a Girl Guide Dressed in Blue" the skipper must catch the rope by standing on it at the last "zoop":

. . . Sailor boys are so funny
This is the way they earn their money:

Zoopa la la
Zoopa la la
Zoop zoop zoop!

In plain skipping another matter must be considered. As far as the skipper is concerned, there are two sides to a turning rope. It depends which side you happen to be standing on when you are about to jump in. The rope may be falling towards you (that's the "plainie side)", or it may be rising away from you (that's the "dykie [wall] side)." In the game of "plainie-dykie," two girls keep jumping in and out, one "plainie" from one side and one "dykie" from the other):

Mrs Red

◇ Mrs Red
Went to bed
In the morning
She was dead.

Most skipping is done using a single rope. In "French Ropes" two ropes are brought into play, each turning inwards. "Down in the Valley" is a favourite song for "Frenchies":

Down in the valley
Where the green grass grows. . . .

In "German Ropes" use is also made of two ropes. One is turned while the other is laid along the ground, or instead a line may be drawn with chalk. The girls "ca'in' " the rope usually keep the one that's on the ground taut and straight by standing on the ends. The skipper has to keep jumping from one side of this rope (or line) to the other. If she fails to do so or touches the rope or trips, she's out.

I'm a little orphan girl
My mother she is dead,
My father is a drunkard
And won't buy me my bread. . . .

In both French ropes and German ropes the rope turns at a
normal pace. But the single skipping-rope may be turned at
quicker rates. Long ago a fast rope was nearly always classed
as a "porridgie." For the last thirty years the term "pepper"
has ousted this.

High Low Dolly Pepper

✧ "The game we play is 'High, low, dolly, pepper!' We keep on
saying:

> High, low, dolly, pepper

until the skipper trips. If she trips at 'High,' the rope's held high
and she has to jump high. If she trips at 'low,' the rope's kept
low and she has to crouch. If she trips at 'dolly,' she has to go
low down and turn round in circles and if she trips at 'pepper,'[4]
you've to turn the rope as fast as you can."

A similar game is played to this couplet, the first line to a slow
rope, the second line to a very fast rope:

> Cup, saucer, plate,
> High, low, dolly, pepper.

Here we have an interesting variation: when the player does
"dolly," she skips in the ordinary way while the "ca'ers" of
the rope circle round her.

One of the most popular forms of skipping today is called
"Skipping with Bumps" or just "Bumps." In Dundee and
elsewhere it is known as "Fireys." In common, plain, or beat
skipping, when you jump off the ground, the rope passes
under your feet *once* every jump, but in bumps it passes *twice*.
In rhymes for bumps this usually happens on the word at the
end of every line, but it might occur on the word at the end
of every second line, and sometimes the bumps are taken on
the words in the middle of each line. Here are three examples
(where the skipper takes bumps the words are in italics):

4 "Pepper" in Edinburgh becomes "vinegar" in the streets of Paris.
Coppée writes in his short story *La Robe Blanche* (1882): ". . . les soirs d'été,
la petite fille qui saute en demandant 'du vinaigre' s'arrête pour me laiser
enjamber la corde."

Ali Baba

❖ Ali Baba and the Forty *Thieves*
Went to school with dirty *knees*
The teacher said: "Stand at *ease*"
Ali Baba and the Forty *Thieves.*

Up & Down

❖ Up and down, up and down
All the way to London *Town*
Leg swing, leg swing
All the way to Ber*lin*
Swish swosh, swish swosh
All the way to King's *Cross*
Heel toe, heel toe
All the way to Mexi*co*
Knees bend, knees bend
All the way to West *End*
March on, march on
All the way to Hong *Kong*
Clap hands, clap hands
All the way to *Pres-ton-pans*!

In the Dark Dark World

❖ In the *dark dark* world
There's a *dark dark* country. . . .

The bumps action halts and therefore emphasises the words concerned. In the case of "Up and Down" the skipper has also to comply with every action mentioned from "leg swing" to "clap hands." For "swish swosh," she keeps both feet close together and jumps from side to side. During the jumping for bumps when the rope has to turn so much faster it sends out a characteristic whining sound. In this rhyme there are six opportunities for bumps:

You Naughty Boy

❖ You naughty *boy*
You stole my *toy*
You named it *Roy*
You naughty *B O Y*!

I

But supposing the skipper wants to do more, she therefore calls out "continues!" and the girls turning the rope supply further fast turnings. The idea is to see how many extra bumps the skipper can accomplish. An alternative way of playing is this. After doing the first six bumps one at a time, "onesers," she can follow with two bumps at a time, "twosers," then "threesers," "foursers," "fivesers" and "sixsers." Next she goes down the scale to "onesers" again.

Games with jumping ropes not only show a high standard of ingenious variation, even their titles have a poetry of their own:

Building-Up the Castle

❧ "Some folk cry [call] it 'heights.' Ye start wi' the rope low doun [down] touching the groond [ground]. Then every time the players do a new jump you heighten the rope, and ye keep on heightening it, until they cannie [can't] jump it." For every new jump the rope should remain at the same height. But if some girl thinks it's rather higher for her than for the others she goes up to the rope and then from underneath she starts clapping her rising hands one over the other and saying: "My-mother-says-the-rope-should-be-this-height!"

Running through the Moon

❧ "Two girls turn the rope for the others. First of all, the skippers run 'right through the moon,' that is, under the rope, one after another. Then they come back to the starting point, the rope turns right round, the leader jumps once, the rest follow suit. Then the leader comes round to jump twice, the rest following, and they dae [do] three and so on. Any's a number can play."

Snakes

❧ A very old game. One player kneels while she "snakes" or undulates the rope. The rest have to jump over this and the first to trip or stand on the rope has then to take her turn of doing the "snaking."

Tidal Waves

❧ In "Tidal Waves," or "Waves," the rope is swayed from side to side by two players, each holding one end.

"Ye swing the rope and the skippers jump over it and each time the rope is raised higher and higher and swings more and more until ye cannie [can't] jump."

Round Rope Heights

✧ In "Round Rope Heights," or "Roundie Heights," a game for several players, "ye stand in the middle and birl [twirl] round with a loose rope in your hand. The others have to jump over it. Ye start wi' the rope at your feet at first, then ye raise it higher and higher till one person trips and they've to birl the rope."

American Ropes

✧ During the early 1960s this game began to catch on in some streets. A long length of elastic is looped round the ankles of two girls who stand opposite each other:

"The girl that's off her end [isn't holding the elastic] stands sidie-ways to the two elastics, puts her foot in the middle, brings it out again, then carries the near elastic over the second elastic with the point of her toe, and brings it out again without touching the second elastic. Ye do that ten times with your right foot, then on the other side you do it ten times with your left foot. Then from each side you do it with both feet together."

Since 1960 the complications of American Ropes have escalated. Generally, it's called "Chinese Ropes" and very often "Elastications"—a rather clever name since the somewhat lengthy elastic has to be contrived by joining together a good number of small, rubber bands. And the loop is now raised in four stages. "Ankles," "Knees," "Waisties and "Headies." But how do wee-er players master "Headies?" By entering the loop *via* a hand-stand or by doing a cartwheel!

There are some hundreds of skipping rhymes and chants, and many of them require from the skippers special skills which are linked with the words used. A selection follows.

Skipping Songs

Climbing up the Ladder

❖ Climbing up the ladder
In a caravan
You only pay a sixpence
To see a funny man;

The funny man choked
Tied to a rope
Ukelele ukelele
Hop hop hop!

You skip up the "ladder"—that is, from one end of the rope to the other until "Ukelele ukelele," after which you hop. Another version starts "Up and down the ladder," and the fifth line: "The funny man broke."

Down in the Valley

❖ Down in the valley
Where the green grass grows,
Where Mary Gray
She grows like a rose:

She grows, she grows,
She grows so sweet
That she calls for her lover
At the end of the street:

Sweetheart, sweetheart
Will you marry me?
Yes, love, yes, love
At half-past three,

Ice cakes, spice cakes
All for tea,
And we'll have a wedding
At half-past three.

Pump, pump, here comes the taxi-cab,
Pump, pump, here comes the taxi-cab,
Pump, pump, here comes the taxi-cab,
Ready for the wedding at half-past three!

Plain skipping. Often used for French ropes.

Down in Yonder Meadow

❖ Down in yonder meadow
Where the green grass grows,
Where Chrissie Fraser
Bleaches her clothes.

She sang, she sang
She sang so sweet
That she sang Johnny Sutherland
Across the street.

Oh he kissed her, he cuddled her
He put her on his knee
And said "dearest Chrissie
I hope we will agree.

Agree, agree,
I hope we will agree
And when we are married
I hope we will agree."

Ropes. Also a ring-game.

Down in the Valley

❖ Down in the valley
Where the green grass grows
There stands a washing lady
Washing her clothes.

With a rubbie-dub here,
And a rubbie-dub there,
That's how the washing lady
Washes her clothes!

Skipping with actions.

Mrs Macaroni

❖ Here comes Mrs Macaroni
Riding on her snow-white pony
Through the streets of Babylonie
This is Marion's wedding day.

Pom pom Susie-anna
Pom pom Susie-anna
Pom pom Susie-anna
This is Marion's wedding day.

Tune: *In and Out the Dusting Bluebells.*

During first verse skipper does actions, during second she hops and "birls [twirls]" or does the "scissors [a cross-legs step]." Sometimes Mrs Macaroni rides on a "silver pony" and "Through the streets of Aberdonie."

I Used to Live

✧ I ula-used to li-li-live in Yalla-lankie, Shalla-lankie
Yalla-lankie, Shalla-lankie, *low*
I ula-used to li-li-live in Yalla-lankie, Shalla-lankie
Yalla-lankie, Shalla-lankie, *go*!

Plain skipping. On approaching "low," the rope dips and the skipper crouches. The rope then rises and at "go!" the skipper jumps out. Often chosen for follow-my-leader games.

I Wish the Night

✧ I wish the night was Saturday night
Tomorrow will be Sunday:
I'll be dressed in all my best
To go out with my Johnny.

Johnny likes to kiss the girls
And Sandy likes to cuddle them,
One, two, three—the boys are after me,
Four, five, six—they're after me with sticks,
Seven, eight, nine—they kiss me all the time,
Ten, eleven, twelve—hurrah! hurrah! hurrah!

Plain skipping.

I'm a Little Orphan Girl

✧ I'm a little orphan girl
My mother she is dead:
My father is a drunkard
And won't buy me my bread.

I sit upon the window sill
To hear the organ play
And think of my dear mother
Who's dead and far away.

Ding, dong, my castle bell
Farewell to my mother
Bury me in the old churchyard
Beside my eldest brother.

My coffin shall be white
Six little angels by my side
Two to sing and two to play
And two to carry my soul away.

A favourite for German ropes.

The Monster of Loch Ness

⟡ I'm the Monster of Loch Ness
My name you'll never guess,
I can sit in a chair
And comb my hair,
I'm the Monster of Loch Ness.

Skipping with actions. "Nessie" can also "sit in the sun" and "eat a bun."

Inky-pinkie . . .

⟡ Inky-pinkie skinny-ma-linkie
Andy-pandy pandy-Andy bandy-boots,
Over-dover dover-rover,
Andy-pandy pandy-Andy bandy-boots!

Plain ropes. Tune: *K-K-K-Katie, K-K-K-Katie.*

A Sweetheart in America

⟡ I've a sweetheart in America
I've another in Dundee-i-ee-i-ee,
I've another in Australia
And that's the one that's going to marry-me-i-ee-i-ee.

First he took me to America
Second he took me to Dundee-i-ee-i-ee,
Third he ran away and left me
Wi' three wee bairns on ma knee-i-ee-i-ee.

One was sittin' on the table
The other was sittin' on ma knee-i-ee-i-ee,
The other was standin' by the door side
Singin': "Daddy will ye no come back tae me-i-ee-i-ee?"

A long-popular skipping song. The tune derives from *What a Friend we Have in Jesus.*

My Girl's a Corker

My girl's a corker
She's a New Yorker,
I'd do most anything
To keep her in style:
She's got a pair of feet
Just like two plates of meat,
That's where all my money goes—
Umpa umpa umpa pa pa
Umpa umpa umpa pa pa.

. . . a pair of shoulders
Just like two great big boulders. . . .

. . . a pair of hips
Just like two battleships. . . .

. . . a great big nose
Just like a fireman's hose.

. . . a pair of eyes
Just like two custard pies.

. . . a head of hair
Just like a grizzly bear.

. . . a pair of legs
Just like two whisky kegs.

. . . a pair of lips
Just like two greasy chips.

This song is used for dancing as well as skipping.

My Faither's Dinner

My mother *a*cried me up to go wi' my faither's   *a called*
    dinner-O:
*b*Champit tatties, beef and steak, three red herrins   *b mashed*
    and a *c*hapnie cake.   *c ha'penny*

I came to a river and I couldnie get across
I paid ten shillings for an old blind horse:
I jumped on its back and its bones went crack
We all played the fiddle till the boat came back.

The boat came back, we all jumped in
The boat capsized and we all fell in.

This skipping-song was heard more in the days before 1914.
But many girls today know it: "Wir [our] grannies lernt
[taught] us." There are therefore a number of slight variations
from "My mither said that A [I] wis to go . . ." to "My
mother said that I must go . . ." The herrings vary from two
to three, the ha'penny cake becomes an oatmeal cake, and
occasionally the horse is black and costs five guineas:

> . . . I up on his back and away with a crack
> And told my mither I'd never come back!

> . . . I jumped on its back and its bones gave a crack
> So *a*A played ma fiddle till the bones came back!   *a I*

The Gipsies in the Wood

⟡ My mother said I never should
Play with the gipsies in the wood
They tugged my hair and broke my comb
I'll tell my mother when I get home.

In the Trinity district the words of the last two lines used to be:

> With an alpaca bodice and a white lace shawl
> A pea-green bonnet and a pink parasol.

An older version of this same skipping tune began:

> I'll tell *a*ma ma when I get home   *a my mother*
> The boys won't leave the girls alone . . .

Wattie Manson

⟡ O Wattie Manson, I am ashamed of you
For leaving Daisy Miller across the ocean blue:
Her heart is nearly broken, she's dying for a kiss—
O Wattie Manson, I am ashamed of this!

Plain skipping, bringing in the skipper's name and also her
sweetheart's. Also a ring game.

Phyllis Hay

⟡ Phyllis Hay on the shore
She has children three and four,
The eldest one is twenty-four
And married to a:
Tinker, tailor,
Soldier, sailor,
Rich man, poor man,
Beggarman, thief!

Plain ropes, with each skipper discovering the occupation of her future son-in-law.

The Wee Wee Woman & the Wee Wee Man

⋄ The wee wee woman and the wee wee man
The wee wee kettle and the wee wee pan
Said the wee wee woman to the wee wee man
You take the kettle and I'll take the pan.

After the "wee wee' woman, man, kettle and pan, we get the "medium-sized", the "tall tall", the "fat fat," the "hopping," the "dancing" and in the seventh and last verse the "jumping" woman, man, kettle and pan.

Skipping with actions. Also popular as a ballie.

Vote, Vote, Vote

⋄ Vote, vote, vote for Janet Reidie
In comes Elsie at the door
She's the one
That gives us all the fun
So we don't want Janet any more
Shut the door.

Plain skipping with Janet Reidie in. She is replaced by Elsie and the skipping verse becomes:

Vote, vote, vote for Elsie Storrie . . .

and so on until all the players get a chance.

SKIPPING-CHANTS

Skipping-chants mostly are spoken in a sing-song style.

All in Together

⋄ All in together
Like a bunch of feathers
One, two, three.

All out together
Like a bunch of feathers
One, two, three.

One skipper jumps in at "one," a second at "two," a third at "three," and at the appropriate time jumps out again.

All in Together Girls

✧ All in together, girls
This fine weather, girls
When I tell your birthday
Please jump in:
January, February, March. . . .

A game for a "big rope." The skippers jump in at their birthday months and in a second verse they "Please jump out." Some players chant only the "jump in" verse and at the end of "December" everybody jumps out.

The Battle of Waterloo

✧ At the Battle of Waterloo
This is what the soldiers do:
Left right left right
All the way to Timbuctoo!

You hop and thrust out your right or left leg rather in a goose-step fashion.

Baby in the Cradle

✧ Baby in the cradle
Playing with the ladle:
One, two, three.

The rope is held high and turned in a smaller circle above a kneeling girl who skips as the rope turns fully at "One, two, three," and then the players go on to chant:

Andy-pandy
Sugarallie-andy:
One, two, three.

—when the skipper jumps out and the rope goes back to where it started from and the next girl comes in to kneel down.

Charlie Chaplin

✧ Charlie Chaplin went to France
To teach the French girls how to dance,
First you do the rumba,
Then you do the kick,
Then you do the turn-about,
Then you do the splits.

Skipping with actions.

Cherry Cherry Cherry-Wine

➤ Cherry cherry cherry-wine
Come back here or I'll tan your *a*hine.   *a hide*

This is one of the rhymes used in the game of "Ten and a Journey." Two girls turn the rope while the rest line up to jump in. The first in does ten ordinary skips, then the rhyme starts, a second girl jumps in while the first jumps out. She now runs round various points and then races back to join in the skipping again. Meanwhile the second skipper has stayed in to finish the rhyme and also to do ten ordinary skips. A third now jumps in as she jumps out and so the game goes on. "Ten and a Journey" can also be played without any rhyme.

"Ye jist coont [count] up to ten as ye skip, jump oot and go a journey roond a car or something and ye have to be back in time to get in the rope before the last lassie has left, otherwise ye're out."

Christopher Columbie-a

➤ Christopher Columbie-a
Sailed across the sea,
And the waves grew higher
And higher and higher and over:
January February March . . .

The rope is swayed back and forward and gradually raised. At "and over" it makes a full turn, and the skipper jumps out at her birthday month.

High Low Dolly Pepper

➤ Cup saucer plate
High low dolly pepper.

The first line is spoken to a slow rope. Then the rope is turned very fast and the second line repeated and repeated until the skipper trips. Everyone gets her turn and remembers what word she tripped at. Then they queue up and do either high, low, dolly, or pepper, and find out how many turns of the rope they can perform. The two lowest performers have to hold the rope in the next game. High, low, and pepper are done as described in "High Low Dolly Pepper," but here, at "dolly," the rope turners move in a circle round the skipper. Of course, if any skipper trips at "Cup saucer plate," she's out and has to hold her end.

House to Let

⬦ House to let
Apply within:
As I go out
A lady comes in.

A rhyme for a follow-my-leader game.

How Many?

⬦ How many messages can I carry?

After having invited your best friend or friends to jump in with you, you try to find the answer to the question by skipping. The skipper may also enquire:

How many baskets will I take with me?
How much change will I get back?
How many shillings will I be short?
How many [a]messages did I drop?   *[a] goods or articles bought*

In fact a multitude of shopping problems can be treated in this way.

I had a Little Dolly

⬦ I had a little dolly
And its name was Bliss:
It took a little jump
And it stopped like this.

This skipping-game starts with the chanting of "January February March," and at the skipper's birthday month it switches over to the rhyme. On reaching the word "this," the skipper has to catch the rope between her legs. If she doesn't succeed, she has to take her end. There are many variants of the rhyme.

I Love Coffee

⬦ I love coffee, I love tea
I like you in with me
I hate coffee, I hate tea
I hate you in with me.

Plain skipping invitation to jump in and then rejection.

I Know a Nigger Boy

✧ I know a nigger boy and he is double-jointed:
He gave me a kiss and I was disappointed,
He gave me another to match the other—
Now, now Chrissie Bathgate, I'll tell your mother
For kissing Willie Hunter a-down by the river:

How many kisses did you give him last night?
One, two, three, four. . . .

Plain skipping. "Chrissie Bathgate" skips until she trips and so the number of kisses is discovered.

I Love Coffee

✧ I love coffee, I love tea
I love the boys and the boys love me,
I wish my mother would hold her tongue,
For she loved the boys when she was young.

Ordinary skipping.

I'm a Girl Guide

✧ I'm a Girl Guide
Dressed in blue
See all the actions
I can do.

Salute to the east
And bow to the west
And turn my back on the sailor boys.

Sailor boys are so funny
This is the way they earn their money:
Zoopa la-la
Zoopa la-la
Zoop zoop zoop!

Skipping with actions and at the last "zoop" the skipper has to catch the rope by standing on it. Instead of "Sailor boys" we often hear "German boys," and instead of "zoopa la-la" often "oopa la-la," with the ending "oop oop oop!"

A Girl Guide Dressed in Green

✧ I'm a Girl Guide dressed in green,
My mother didn't want me
So she sent me to the Queen:

The Queen didn't want me
So she sent me to the King,
The King said: "Shut your eyes
And count sixteen."

Ordinary skipping. The skipper does sixteen jumps with her
eyes shut.

A Little Brownie Girl

✧ I'm a little Brownie girl
Dressed in brown,
See my knickers hanging down:
Pull them up, pull them down!
I'm a little Brownie girl
Dressed in brown.

Skipping with actions.

Ice-Cream & Jelly

✧ Inky pinkie
Sugarallie inkie:
One two three!

Ice-cream and jelly
A punch on the belly:
One two three!

Plain skipping with jumping in and out.

Jelly on the Plate

✧ Jelly on the plate,
Jelly on the plate:
Wiggle-waggle, wiggle-waggle—
Jelly on the plate.

Sausage in the pan,
Sausage in the pan:
Turn it round, turn it round—
Sausage in the pan.

Paper on the floor,
Paper on the floor:
Pick it up, pick it up—
Paper on the floor.

Baby in the pram,
Baby in the pram:
Pull her out, pull her out—
Baby in the pram.

Burglars in the house,
Burglars in the house:
Kick 'em out, kick 'em out—
Burglars in the house.

At the verses concerned, the skipper wiggle-waggles, birls round, pretends to pick up the paper, rocks her arms, and kicks out her legs.

Kings & Queens

✧ Kings and Queens
And partners two,
All dressed up in
Royal blue:

One two
How do you do?

I do very well
With a *a*house to *b*masel':   *a* pron. *hooss*   *b* *myself*
A door and a bell
And a coconut shell:
One two three!

The "Kings" stand beside one end of the rope, the "Queens" by the other. As the rhyme starts a King jumps in at "Kings" and a Queen at "Queens." They skip plain and at "One two, How do you do?" they shake hands and then change places. Skipping continues until both jump out at "One two three!" The rhyme varies a lot, especially the last three lines:

A key to my door
A number four:
One two three!

Lady Lady

✧ Lady, lady, drop your hanky
Lady, lady, pick it up:
Lady, lady, spell your name
N A N C Y   S M A I L.

Skipping with actions.

Matthew Mark

✧ Matthew Mark Luke and John
*a*Hud the *b*cuddie till I get on: *a* hold *b* horse
Hud him fast, hud him steady—
Hud him like a *c*Finnan huddie.   *c* Findon haddock

Matthew Mark Luke and John
Hud the cuddie: I'm on
I'm on, the cuddie's gone—
Matthew Mark Luke and John.

Plain skipping.

The Toffee Shop

✧ Maureen had a toffee shop
And Susan came a-buying:
Susan took a whirly kick
And sent poor Maureen flying.

Skipping with actions. Maureen skips in her "toffee shop";
Susan jumps in and kicks her out. Susan now runs the business
till a new customer appears.

My Little Dolly

✧ My little dolly dressed in blue
Died last night at half-past-two,
I put her in the coffin
She fell through the bottom,
My little dolly dressed in blue.

Plain skipping. Also used as ballie.

Nebuchadnezzar

✧ Nebuchadnezzar, King of the Jews
Sold his wife for a pair of shoes.
When the shoes began to wear
Nebuchadnezzar began to swear,
When the swearing began to stop
Nebuchadnezzar bought a shop,
When the shop began to sell
Nebuchadnezzar bought a bell,
When the bell began to ring
Nebuchadnezzar began to sing:
One two three:
Doh ray me
Fah soh la te doh!

K

Plain ropes. There is no mention of Nebuchadnezzar's trans-
action in the Bible, although according to Amos, II. 6, "they
sold . . . the poor for a pair of shoes." Instead of Nebuchadnezzar the name may be "Eli Canessa" or "Kenneth Macalpine"
or "Scottie-ma-lottie" or "Archie-ball-ball-ball," a well-known
bumps rhyme.

All Good Children

✧ One two three four five six seven
All good children go to heaven:
When they die their sin's forgiven—
One two three four five six seven.

Plain skipping. The last two lines often appear as:

Penny on the water, tuppence on the sea,
Thruppence on the railway, and out goes she!

Over the Mountain

✧ Over the mountain
Over the sea
Johnny broke a ᵃwindie   ᵃ *window*
And blamed it on me.

I told my ma
My ma told my dad,
Johnny got a leathering
Ha! ha! ha!

Plain ropes.

Red, White & Blue

✧ Red, white, and blue
My mother's caught the flu:
My faither's lost his walking stick—
And I blame you!

Ordinary skipping. The skippers enjoy the fun of pointing at
one of their friends. The one pointed at is the next skipper.

Stars

✧ Roy Rodgers
Betty Grable
Rita Hayworth
Clark Gable.

Each skipper in turn mimicks the four film stars.

Salt Pepper

✧ "Ye start off skippin', wi' the two that ca' the rope going as fast as they can and keepin' on saying 'Salt, pepper, mustard, vinegar!' If ye stop at 'salt,' ye lower yoursel' as ye skip for ten turns. If ye stop at 'pepper,' ye've tae skip right fast for ten turns. If ye stop at 'mustard,' ye've to turn round low down for ten turns. If ye stop at 'vinegar,' ye circle for ten turns."

The French artist Marie Laurencin (even as a young woman) was very keen on her jumping ropes, and the poet Guillaume Apollinaire has described her visits to him. She'd come along skipping and later on when she left she'd skip downstairs, stopping at the gate to do "une vinaigrette" (three fast turns) which apparently meant "Goodbye. See you soon! See you tomorrow!"[5]

Standing at the Bar

✧ Standing at the bar
Smoking a cigar
Riding on a donkey
Ha! Ha! Ha!
Take my arm
I do no harm
I only smoke a cigar.

Skipping with actions.

Teddy-Bear Teddy-Bear

✧ Teddy-bear, Teddy-bear, twirl around
Teddy-bear, Teddy-bear, touch the ground
Teddy-bear, Teddy-bear, show your shoe
Teddy-bear, Teddy-bear, that will do.

Teddy-bear, Teddy-bear, climb upstairs
Teddy-bear, Teddy-bear, say your prayers
Teddy-bear, Teddy-bear, put out the light
Teddy-bear, Teddy-bear, say goodnight.
Goodnight!

Skipping with actions.

[5] Cecily Mackworth, *Guillaume Apollinaire and the Cubist Movement* (1961).

There She Goes

⋄ There she goes, there she goes
Like an elephant on her toes
Look at her feet, she thinks she's neat
Black stockings and dirty feet.

A follow-my-leader. For "one no miss" the first skipper jumps
in for the first line and then out, the second for the second line
and so on. In "two no miss" the skippers in quick succession
have to skip for the first line, two for the second and so on, only
for the last line the two stay in for the whole length of the line.
They jump for the four beats and then out. The same happens
with "four no miss" when four skippers take up each line.

This Year, Next Year

⋄ This Year
Next year
Sometime
Never.

This is a famous skipping chant also used as a ballie, or for a
game on paper, or for playing with cherry or other fruit stones.
If you trip or fall at "never," you are of course out the game:
but if you are still in, then "*A B C* . . ." decides the letters of
your husband's name; "tinker, tailor, soldier, sailor," his
occupation; "Monday, Tuesday . . ." the day of the week on
which you'll be married; "silk, rayon, cotton, rags," what
you'll wear; "stolen, borrowed, bought, or given," how you
will have acquired it; "motor car, barrie [barrow], scooter,
dung cart," what you'll drive in; "big house, wee house, pig
stye, pre-fab," where you'll live; and "one, two, three . . .,"
the number of children you'll have.

Up in the North

⋄ Up in the North
A long way off
A donkey caught
The whooping cough.

What shall we give him
To make him better?
Salt mustard
Vinegar pepper.

The last two lines are repeated and repeated, making a skipping
game similar to "Salt Pepper Mustard Vinegar."

Yankie Pankie

✧ Yankie pankie sugarallie-ankie
One two three
Baby in the cradle
Playing with the ladle:
One two three
Yankie pankie sugarallie-ankie
One two three.

Another version of "Baby in the Cradle."

Songs and Chants for Bumps

When the successful skipper reaches the end of most of these rhymes, either she asks for more bumps by calling out "Continues!" or she elects to play "Twosers," "Threesers," right up to "Sixsers." This means that the rhyme is repeated six times, and at every repetition she does an extra bump. After "sixsers" she tries to go down the scale to "onesers" again.

"I like bumps because there's mair fast actions, it's mair difficult, and so ye get mair o' a shot [more chances]."

Ali Baba

✧ Ali Baba and his Forty *Men*
Went to school at half-past-*ten*:
The teacher said "Late *again!*"
Ali Baba and his Forty *Men*.

Archibal'

✧ Archie-*ball-ball-ball*
King of the *Jews-Jews-Jews*
Sellt his *wife-wife-wife*
For a pair of *shoes-shoes-shoes*.

When the *shoes-shoes-shoes*
Began to *wear-wear-wear*
Archie-*ball-ball-ball*
Began to *swear-swear-swear*.

When the *swear-swear-swear*
Began to *stop-stop-stop*
Archie-*ball-ball-ball*
Bought a *shop-shop-shop*.

When the *shop-shop-shop*
Began to *sell-sell-sell*
Archie-*ball-ball-ball*
Bought a *bell-bell-bell*.

When the *bell-bell-bell*
Began to *ring-ring-ring*
Archie-*ball-ball-ball*
Began to *sing-sing-sing*,

Doh ray me fah
Soh lah te doh,
Who stole my wife
I do not know!

This new variation of "Nebuchadnezzar, King of the Jews," so admirably suited to bumps skipping, first appeared in Edinburgh in the spring of 1945. Street after street could be heard taking it up. Even boys chanted it too—out of sheer enthusiasm for its vigorous rhythm. The last four lines are sung.

Big Ben

✧ Big Ben strikes *one*
Big Ben strikes *two*
Big Ben strikes *three* . . .

and so on, up to ". . . *twelve*."

Hokey Pokey

✧ Hokey pokey penny-a-*lump*
That's the stuff to make you *jump*.
One
    Two
       Three. . . .

After "jump," the skipper calls "Continues!" and finds how many bumps she can accomplish. Some streets simply say "Ice-cream penny-a-*lump*."

In Edinburgh in the 1880s ice-cream was sold almost solely by Italians who paraded the streets with handcarts. Their cry was:

Hokey pokey penny-a-lump
That's the stuff to make you jump!

The ice-cream (oblong in shape) was wrapped in pure white paper. It was considered to be very cold. "Hokey pokey" may come from "hocus pocus" or perhaps from the Neapolitan pronunciation of "*Ecco un poco*," meaning *here's a little!*"

The Little Sausage

✧ I had a little *sausage*
A dear little *sausage*:
I put it in the *oven*
For my *tea-tea-tea*.

I went out to *play*
And I heard the sausage *say*:
"Come in little *lassie*
For your *tea-tea-tea*."

I Know a Scout

✧ I know a *Scout*
Who took me *out*:
He gave me *chips*
To grease my *lips*:
He gave me *kisses*
One
    Two
        Three. . . .

The skipper shouts "Continues!" and counts the bumps as kisses.

Rubber Knickers

✧ I wore rubber knickers
Until I was
One two three . . .

Or it might be a "bib" or a "feeder."

Lady in Tight Skirt

✧ Lady in the tight skirt
  Can't do *this*:
Lady in the tight skirt
Can't do *this*:
Lady in the tight skirt
Can't do *this*—
        This
That
        This
That. . . .

A bumps with "Continues!"

My Big Red Ball

✧ My big red *ball*
   Went over the *wall*
   I told my *mum*   *a slapped*
   She ᵃskelpt my *bum*
   B U M.

Gipsies in the Wood

✧ My mother *said* that I never *should*
   Play with the *gipsies* in the *wood*:
   If I *did*, she would *say*
   "You naughty, naughty *girl* to diso*bey*
   Diso*bey*, *di*sobey, naughty girl to *di*sobey."

Nelly the Elephant

✧ Nelly the elephant packed her *trunk*
   And said goodbye to the *circus*
   Off she went with a trumpety-*trump*
   Trump, trump, trump!

Oliver

✧ Oliver *Jump*
   Oliver *Jump*
   Oliver *Jump Jump Jump*!

   Oliver *Kick*
   Oliver *Kick*
   Oliver *Kick Kick Kick*!

   Oliver *Twist*
   Oliver *Twist*
   Oliver *Twist Twist Twist*!

   Oliver *Jump, Jump Jump*
   Kick Kick Kick
   Twist Twist Twist!

Bumps with actions. Very, very popular. Every skipper tries to make her shot turn out a triumph for her own, unique, versatility.

O Wilma Ballantyne

✧ O Wilma Ballantyne why did you run away
   And leave your darling Bobby across the ocean sea?

His heart is nearly broken, he's dying for a kiss—
O Wilma Ballantyne, I'll tell your mother this.
Kiss
    Kiss
        Kiss
            Kiss. . . .

"Continues!" is called to count the kisses.

Policeman Policeman

Policeman, policeman, don't blame *me*
Blame that boy behind the *tree*:
He stole sugar, he stole *tea*—
Policeman, policeman, don't blame *me*.

P.K. Chewing Gum

P.K. Chewing Gum
Penny per *packet*
First you chew it
Then you *crack it*
Then you stick it
In your *jacket*.
Then your mother
Kicks up a *racket*
P.K. Chewing Gum
Penny per *packet*.

Queen Elizabeth

Queen Elizabeth lost her *shoe*
At the Battle of Water*loo*
It happened on a *Monday*
         Tuesday
           Wednesday. . . .

"Continues!" is called here to see how many weeks of bumps
the skipper can do.

Rabbie Burns

Rabbie Burns was born in *Ayr*
Now he's in Trafalgar *Square*
If ye want tae see him *there*
Jump on a bus and skip the *fare*.

For bumps we have a second verse which becomes:

> Rabbie Burns was born in *Ayr, Ayr*
> Now he's in Trafalgar *Square, Square* . . .

And a third:

> Rabbie Burns was born in *Ayr, Ayr, Ayr* . . .

In this way the tune grows a little longer and sounds more curious. It's rather nice to find that the children have made this little rhyme about our national bard all on their own! Here's a laddie's own account of his experience one 25th January:

✧ "A went to a Burns Night. It was right rude. It was a play thing and Rabbie Burns say'd to the lassie: 'Let's go up to the bed.' The lassie says 'Naw!' and aboot half-an-oor later, they're on the stage again, and ye seen the two oan a bed. It was clarty what that play was aboot! Ma auntie wis in it but she wisnie the wumman! Hoo A gote to the place, A dinnie ken, A jist walked into the joint and it was thair!"

Burns is also the hero and speaker of a Rose Street poem:

✧ I'm plain Rabbie Burns
  I work at the ᵃploo . . .   *ᵃ plough*

Raspberry, Strawberry

✧ Raspberry, strawberry, blackcurrant *jam*
  Tell me the name of your young *man*
  A
        B
              C. . . .

"Continues!' here to find the first letter of the boy-friend's name. The skipper tries, of course, to catch the rope between her legs at the letter she wants—and nearly always succeeds!

Robin Hood

✧ Robin Hood and his Merry *Men*
  Went to school at half past *ten*.
  The teacher said "Late *again*!"
  Robin Hood and his Merry *Men*.

Who's Got Feet . . . .

✧ Who's got *feet*
  Like Arthur' *Seat*?

Who's got a *bunion*
Like a pickled *onion*?

Who's got *legs*
Like ham and *eggs*?

Who's got *hips*
Like battle*ships*?

Who's got *eyes*
Like apple *pies*?

Who's got *lips*
Like greasy *chips*?

Who's got a *nose*
Like a big fat *rose*?

Who's got *slippers*
Like great big *kippers*?

Falling

✧ You can fall from a *steeple*
You can fall from *above*:
But for heaven's sake, *Georgina*—
Don't fall in *love*!

You Naughty . . .

✧ You naughty *girl*
You stole my *curl*:
You named it *Twirl*—
You naughty G I R L!

"You Naughty Boy" first set the pattern for these rhymes:

You naughty *lady*
You stole my *baby*:
You named it *Sadie*
You naughty L A D Y!

Skipping rhymes (like all the playing rhymes) must be recognised as *living rhymes*. Some, it's true, may die: but new ones are always being born. As for the rest they make every shift to keep alive. For the last thirty or forty years the "Big Ben" chant hadn't changed in one iota, and now over the past few months it has suddenly started to grow!

> ✧ Big Ben strikes *one*
> Tick tock
> Big Ben strikes *two*
> Tick tock

For "tick tock" the player with her two feet makes a to and fro skip;

Another fresh feature is this skipping academy:

> *The Beatles' School*
> ✧ In the Beatles' *school*
> In Liver*pool*
> They learn their *yea yea yea*:

"Then you do twosers, theesers up to sixsers and after that 'Continues'!"

8

SINGING GAMES

Nearly all the singing games begin with the players standing in a ring or lining up in a row. In most of the ring-games the players keep in a ring from start to finish. But between the ring and the row there's a good deal of interchanging. A game like "In and Out the Dusting Bluebells" begins with a ring, but it ends with the players forming a long chain. In "The Big Ship Sails through the Eely-Alley-O," the players start off in a row, but they finish in a circling ring. In "Chinese Government, Black man's Daughter," the game begins with a line of players, and ends up with a line, but in between, a circling ring plays a most important part. In all these games, too, little "jing-a-rings," or dances between two, are a very common feature. To have collected, over the whole country, all the different versions of even one of these singing games might well have been a labour of Hercules. The tunes hardly differ, but the words vary quite a lot. In Edinburgh even neighbouring streets seem to prefer their own brands of words. This is particularly true of the two ring-games "Poor Tommy is Dead and Laid in his Grave" and "The Wind, the Wind, the Wind Blows High," and also of that famous old row game "There Came three Jews from the Land of Spain."

GAMES PLAYED IN A ROW

Chinese Government

✧ Chinese government[1]
Black man's daughter
Tra-la la-la-la la-la!

---

[1] "Chinese" is an adjective children often clap in front of a word, and it conveys ideas of being odd or sinister or cruel or sort of upside-down or even ununderstandable. But why choose this noun "government?" Well it

The wind blows high
From the sky
And out pops Kitty
With a big black eye!

Girls stand in a line with one girl facing them. Everybody sings; and, as the song is sung, this one girl dances back and forward opposite Kitty, who pops out the line with the mention of her name and circles round her. The song and action are repeated and a second girl (perhaps "Jeanie") comes out and tags on behind Kitty, and now both circle round. This goes on until everybody has been called and all are circling round the one girl. The same girl now dictates the return of the girls to the row again, and the last back is "out" for the next game.

A Bunch of Roses

◇   Chrissie Campbell, fresh and fair
A bunch of roses she shall wear:
Gold and silver by her side—
I know who's her bride.

Take her by the lily-white hand
Lead her across the water:
Give her kisses, one two three—
For she's a lady's daughter.

The players form up in a row with one girl facing them. She advances and retires opposite Chrissie Campbell during singing of first verse. On the first two lines of the second verse Chrissie Campbell is walked around, then the pair cross hands and birl for the rest of the verse. Chrissie Campbell is now out.

Have You any Bread & Wine?

◇   The players line up in two rows. Each advances a few paces, says its verse, and then retreats. At the last verse, both rows advance, and a mock battle takes place.

---

happens to be one of the commonest words young people are liable to overhear either in the house or in the street or in the shops. It also crops up in a game of knocking at a door when this guarded dialogue takes place:

"Who's there?"
"Gover'ment!"
"What's the position?"
"Grim."
"Come in!"

ROW 1:

> Have you any bread and wine?
> We are the rovers:
> Have you any bread and wine?
> For we're the gallant soldiers.

ROW 2:

> Yes, we have some bread and wine
> We are the rovers:
> Yes, we have some bread and wine
> For we're the gallant soldiers.

ROW 1:

> Shall we have one glass of it?
> We are the rovers:
> Shall we have one glass of it?
> For we're the gallant soldiers.

ROW 2:

> One glass of it you shall not have,
> We are the rovers:
> One glass of it you shall not have
> For we're the gallant soldiers.

ROW 1:

> We shall send for the redcoat men
> We are the rovers:
> We shall send for the redcoat men
> For we're the gallant soldiers.

ROW 2:

> What care we for the redcoat men?
> We are the rovers:
> What care we for the redcoat men?
> For we're the gallant soldiers.

ROW 1:

> We shall send for the bluecoat men
> We are the rovers:
> We shall send for the bluecoat men
> For we're the gallant soldiers.

ROW 2:

> What care we for the bluecoat men?
> We are the rovers:
> What care we for the bluecoat men?
> For we're the gallant soldiers.

BOTH ROWS:

> Buckle up your sleeves and we'll have a fight
> We are the rovers:
> Buckle up your sleeves and we'll have a fight
> For we're the gallant soldiers.

Babylon

> ⟡ —How many miles to Babylon?
> —Three score and ten.
> —Shall I be there by candle-light?
> —Yes, and back again!
>
> —Open the gates and let us through!
> —Not without a ᵃbeck and ᵇbou!   *ᵃ curtsey ᵇ bow*
> —There's the beck, there's the bou,
>   Open the gates and let us through!

The players form into two rows facing each other, each row singing its own line. For the "beck" those in Row 1 bend back, and for the "bou" they bow forward. At the demand "Open the gates and let us through!" Those in Row 2 form an arch, through which those in Row 1 rush. Row 1 now become Row 2, the players forming the arch become Row 1 and the game restarts.

This singing game was a great favourite with R. L. S.:

> "Our phantom voices haunt the air
> As we were still at play
> And I can hear them call and say:
> '*How far is it to Babylon.*'"

It is very seldom heard nowadays. This chanted version was played right up to 1914:

SPOKESMAN FOR ROW 1:

> How many miles to Babylon?

ROW 2:

Three score and ten.

SPOKESMAN FOR ROW I:

Shall I be there by candle-light?

ROW 2:

Oh yes, and back again!

SPOKESMAN FOR ROW I:

Then open your gates as high as you like
And let King George and all his Royal Family through!

ROW 2:

Not without the *a*back and the *b*bou!   *a curtsey   b bow*

SPOKESMAN FOR ROW I:

There's the back and there's the bou—
Open the gates and let us through!

Here the players are ranged in two rows facing each other, as
before—only the first row advance to ask each question, and
then they retire to hear the answer from the second row which
always stand still. The first row ask through one spokesman,
while the second row answer in unison. The spokesman for
the first row leans back for the "back" and curtseys for the
"bou." Two players in the middle of the second row then take
hands and form an arch through which the first row and all
the rest pour, holding on to each other's waists and chanting:

One little, two little, three little Indians
Four little, five little, six little Indians
Seven little, eight little, nine little Indians
Ten little Indian boys!

Queen Alexandra

✧ Queen Alexandra has lost her gold ring
Lost her gold ring, lost her gold ring:
Queen Alexandra has lost her gold ring—
And guess who has found it?

The girls stand or sit in a row, eyes shut, and hands held before
them with palms vertical, touching, and almost (but not quite)

L

closed. The one that's out sings the rhyme, and has her palms closed similarly on a ring. While singing, she moves her hands above the other players' hands, she drops the ring between someone else's palms. The player the rhyme ends on has to guess who's got the ring. If she guesses correctly, she takes up the ring, and has her chance of going round; if not, the same girl starts up the same over again.

A fairly common second line is:

> Sent by the King, lost her gold ring

Queen Mary

◇ Queen Mary, Queen Mary, my age is sixteen
My father's a farmer on yonder green:
He's plenty of money to dress me ^asae braw—   *^a so fine*
But ^bnae bonnie laddie will tak' me awa'.   *^b no*

I rose in the morning, I looked in the glass
I said to myself "What a handsome young lass!"
My hands by my side, and I gave a "Ha-ha!"—
For nae bonnie laddie will tak' me awa'.

Girls stand in a row. Another girl stands in front of them; and she sings the first verse. Then during the first two lines of the second verse she faces one of the girls; and at the last two, they do a half circle, and the "bonnie laddie" now takes the place of the "handsome young lass."

See the Robbers Passing by

◇ Having decided which of them is to be "golden," and which "silver," two of the girls clasp hands and raise their arms to form an arch. Each holding on to the one in front of her, all the other girls go under this arch, singing:

ALL:

> See the robbers passing by
> Passing by, passing by:
> See the robbers passing by
> My fair lady!

Then, lowering their arms, the two girls enclose one of the other players, and rock her to and fro, singing:

THE TWO:

What's the robbers done to you
Done to you, done to you?
What's the robbers done to you
My fair lady?

The prisoner replies:

THE PRISONER:

Stole my comb, and lost my shoe
Lost my shoe, lost my shoe:
Stole my comb, and lost my shoe
My fair lady!

Then the two girls tell her:

THE TWO:

Off to prison you must go
You must go, you must go:
Off to prison you must go
My fair lady!

After this, they take the prisoner aside and ask her, "What do you want? A golden shoe or a silver shoe?" And her choice settles which of the two she's to stand behind. When all the other girls have been captured, and have gone to stand behind one of the two, there follows a tug-o'-war between "golden shoes" and "silver shoes"—or, maybe, between golden and silver "oranges," or "apples," or "pears," or "lockets."

The Eely-Alley-O

The big ship sails through the Eely-Alley-O
The Eely-Alley-O, the Eely-Alley-O:
The big ship sails through the Eely-Alley-O—
On the fourteenth of December.

The big ship sails too slow, too slow
Too slow, too slow, too slow, too slow:
The big ship sails too slow, too slow—
On the fourteenth of December.

The Captain said it would never never do
Never never do, never never do:
The Captain said it would never never do—
On the fourteenth of December.

The big ship sails too fast, too fast
Too fast, too fast, too fast, too fast:
The big ship sails too fast, too fast—
On the fourteenth of December.

The players line up in a row, and the first girl at one end places
her hand against a wall, forming an arch. With her other hand
all the rest of the players are linked hand-in-hand. The first
verse is then sung; and, led by the player at the free end, the
big ship proceeds through the Eely-Alley-O (*i.e.*, the arch).
After the last girl has gone through the first girl takes her hand
off the wall, and turns about; and between them these two
form another arch. The row then goes through the second arch.
A third arch is formed, and so on. The players never let go their
clasped hands, so that eventually a ring is formed with hands
intercrossed. The first verse is repeated until this stage is reached.
At the second verse, the ring circles slowly; at the third the
arms go up and down; and at the last they whirl round with the
greatest possible speed. The players usually find themselves
facing inwards, but quite often they're facing outwards, so
that they go round the ring backwards.

The last line of each verse varies considerably. Instead of
"fourteenth" some players sing "first day" or "last day" of
"September" or "November."

There Came Three Jews

One of the players is chosen as a suitor, and the others all line
up in a row, singing:

> There came three Jews
> From the land of Spain
> To call upon
> My sister Jane.

> My sister Jane
> Is far too young:
> I cannot bear
> Her chattering tongue.

Meanwhile the suitor advances in front of them, and they say
(not sing):

> Go away, Corkscrew!

And in reply he says:

> My name is not Corkscrew:
> I stamp my foot
> And away I go!

As he withdraws, the others sing:

> Come back, come back
> Your coat's so green:
> And choose the fairest
> One you seen!

In reply, he sings:

> The fairest one
> That I can see
> Is bonnie wee Jean—
> Will ye come to me?

But she says:

> No!

Turning his back, and kicking his heels, the suitor sings:

> Ye dirty wee rat, ye'll ^ano come oot   ^a *not*
> No come oot, no come oot:
> Ye dirty wee rat, ye'll no come oot
> To help me wi' a my washin'!

Then, doing the same, the others sing:

> The same applies to you, sir,
> To you, sir, to you, sir:
> The same applies to you, sir—
> E-I-O, sir!

Although she has apparently rejected the suitor, "bonnie wee Jean" now joins him; and the game goes on being repeated until all the others, except one, have joined the suitor, and are in a row facing the other way. That one becomes the suitor for the next game. Or else a ring is formed round this last player, and they go round singing:

> Now I've got the Prince of Wales
> The Prince of Wales, the Prince of Wales:
> Now I've got the Prince of Wales
> To help me with my washing.

The Prince of Wales is of course the new suitor. This version is the one that used to be played in Bothwell Street (1938).

In a version played in Restalrig Square (1958), the three Jews are called the "three Dews," and they come from the "Isle of Spain"; the Suitor is not called "Corkscrew," but "Cocksparrow"; and when his "fairest one" comes out, they take hands, and advance and retreat together in front of the row. When only one girl is still left in the row, the others form a ring round her, singing:

> Now we've got the Fairy Queen
> The Fairy Queen, the Fairy Queen:
> Now we've got the Fairy Queen
> To help us with our washing.

The "Fairy Queen" is out for the next game.

"The Three Dukes" or "Jews" or "Dews from Spain" is the same as the game Robert Chambers described in his *Popular Rhymes* (1841) as "We are Three Brethern Come from Spain," which was then sung "to a very sweet air." From the position of his refrains it is clear that the words of his ballad couldn't fit the tune used today. It is remarkable, though, how much of the sense of the thing, and certain words and phrases in some of the verses, have remained:

> We are three brethern come from Spain,
> All in French garlands;
> We've come to court your daughter Jean,
> And adieu to you, my darlings.
>
> My daughter Jean she is too young,
> All in French garlands;
> She cannot bide your flattering tongue,
> And adieu to you, my darlings.
>
> Come back, come back, you courteous knights,
> All in French garlands;
> Clean up your spurs, and make them bright,
> And adieu to you, my darlings.

There is, however, nothing in Chambers's version which gives a clue to that curious command "Go away, Corkscrew!" or "Go away, Cock sparrow!" or (as in a sort of Salvador Dali transformation) "Go away, Cockshoe!"

The Bonnie Bunch of Roses

All the girls except one stand in a row; and she stands in front of them. First they all sing:

> Up against the wall for the London Ball
> The London Ball, the London Ball:
> Up against the wall for the London Ball
> For the Bonnie Bunch of Roses!

Then the girl in front sings:

> Mother, mother, may I go?
> May I go? May I go?
> Mother, mother, may I go
> To the Bonnie Bunch of Roses?

From the row, her mother replies by singing:

> Yes, my darling, you may go,
> You may go, you may go:
> Yes, my darling, you may go
> To the Bonnie Bunch of Roses.

All then sing:

> She buckled up her skirt and away she went
> Away she went, away she went:
> She buckled up her skirt and away she went
> To the Bonnie Bunch of Roses.

> She met her lover on the way
> On the way, on the way:
> She met her lover on the way
> To the Bonnie Bunch of Roses.

> He gave her a kiss, and a one two three
> A one two three, a one two three:
> He gave her a kiss, and a one two three
> To the Bonnie Bunch of Roses.

> She shook her head and said goodbye
> She said goodbye, she said goodbye:
> She shook her head and said goodbye
> To the Bonnie Bunch of Roses.

During the first three verses, the girl advances and retreats. At the third verse she "buckles up her skirt" and circles round alone, and near the end she points at someone, who acts the lover in the next verse when the pair go round holding hands. In the sixth verse, both hold "switchie hands [crossed hands]" and do a "birl [turn]," stopping at "kiss" for a kiss. The lover then goes back to the row, and the girl circles round alone with her right hand raised and shaking her head at each "goodbye."

RING-GAMES

Poor Tommy is Dead

Poor Tommy is dead and laid in his grave
Laid in his grave, laid in his grave!
Poor Tommy is dead and laid in his grave—
A long time ago!

There grew an old apple-tree over his head
Over his head, over his head:
There grew an old apple-tree over his head—
A long time ago!

The apples grew ripe and started to fall
Started to fall, started to fall:
The apples grew ripe and started to fall—
A long time ago!

There came an Old Woman come picking them up
Picking them up, picking them up:
There came an Old Woman come picking them up—
A long time ago!

Poor Tommy got up and he gave her a kick
Gave her a kick, gave her a kick:
Poor Tommy got up and he gave her a kick—
A long time ago!

That made her go off with a skippety hop
A skippety hop, a skippety hop:
That made her go off with a skippety hop—
A long time ago!

"Poor Tommy" lies flat on the ground while the players circle slowly round him (first verse). Someone then takes the part of the apple-tree with their arms raised and drooping over like branches (second verse). These branches now drop their apples to left and to right (third verse). The Old Woman then comes into the ring and starts picking them up (fourth verse). Poor Tommy rises with the greatest speed and ceremonially "kicks" her round and round, and finally out of the ring (fifth and sixth verses). This version is the one sung in Loganlea Place. Here are the first verses sung in three other streets, all in the same area—namely:

(1) in Lochend Quadrant:

> Poor Tommy, poor Tommy is dead in his grave
> Dead in his grave, dead in his grave:
> Poor Tommy, poor Tommy is dead in his grave—
> Tra la la!

(2) in Craigentinny Road:

> Poor Rodger, poor Rodger, he's dead in his grave
> He's dead in his grave, he's dead in his grave:
> Poor Rodger, poor Rodger, he's dead in his grave—
> E I O!

and (3) in Ferrier Street:

> Old Rodger is dead and lies in his grave
> Lies in his grave, lies in his grave:
> Old Rodger is dead and lies in his grave—
> Doh ray me!

Besides these refrains, many others may be heard, such as:

> . . . Oh! Oh! died in his grave!

> . . . Heigh! Ho! laid in his grave!

> . . . All through the night!

> . . . Many years ago!

> . . . Oh! how sad!

> . . . Oh! Oh! Oh!

Shaw's Professor Higgins maintained that he could tell where any Londoner lived simply by listening to his speech: "I can place him within two miles in London. Sometimes within two streets." A street directory of Edinburgh, based on these refrains of "Poor Tommy," could easily be compiled. One or two streets call him "Pure Tommy," and many players introduce into the second verse other fruit-trees besides the apple-tree. You get pear-trees, orange-trees, and banana-trees: but it's only when the apples are being gathered that Tommy resurrects himself. Another way of prolonging the game is for the Old Woman to bring along some of her friends, who help her to collect the various fruits.

Evelyn Nicholson

✧ Evelyn Nicholson on the shore
She has children three and four:
The eldest one is twenty-four—
And married to a sailor.

Ali Baba one two three
Ali Baba *A B C*:
Ali Baba one two three—
And married to a sailor!

Tune: *Alie balie Alie balie bee.*

Girls hand-in-hand form a ring and dance round Evelyn Nicholson in the middle while singing the first verse. They stop at the word "sailor" and Evelyn now dances opposite "him" as the second verse begins. The pair may do a *pas-de-bas* or a leg-kick or a leg-swing, take arms, or take hands, or skip, as they go round. The "sailor" now stands in the circle. Another version supplies this alternative for the last line of the second verse:

. . . And married to a tinker, tailor, soldier, sailor,
Rich man, poor man, beggarman, thief!

And Evelyn does a *pas-de-bas* right round the circle with her finger pointing until she arrives at the thief who is the next to go in the middle.

Halliballoo Ball-aye

✧ Halliballoo balloo
Halliballoo ball-aye:
Halliballoo balloo—
Upon a Saturday night!

Put your right foot in
Put your right foot out:
Shake it a little, a little—
And turn yourself about.

For the first verse you join hands and circle round. At the
second verse everybody stops and puts in their right foot
towards centre of circle, then to the outside of circle, and
turning round on the words "turn yourself about." Then hands
are linked again for another verse of the chorus whose last line
is often sung: "Upon a Saturday night—hooch!"[2] After right
foot come left foot, right hand, left hand, right arm, left arm,
right ear, left ear, wee nose, right eye, left eye, finishing with
"whole self."

A Poor Widow

Here's a poor widow, she's left alone
She has no money to marry upon—
Come choose to the East
Come choose to the West
Come choose to the one that you love best.

Now they're married and we wish them joy
Every year a girl and boy—
Loving each other
Like sister and brother
To play the game at kissing-the-gether.

For the first verse the girls dance round the Widow in the
centre, who picks her "sweetheart." The second verse then
starts up, the two in the centre kiss—and then the game begins
again with the Sweetheart as the new widow. This is the same
"Widow of Babylon" whom Robert Chambers recorded in
his *Popular Rhymes*. Hers is a fabulous and ancient widowhood
which has every prospect of being enacted for a long time to
come.

The Blue Bird

Here comes the blue bird through my window
Here comes the blue bird through my door:
Here comes the blue bird through my window—
Hi diddle um dum dee.

[2] A Highland dancer's shout.

Take a little dance and hop in the corner
Take a little dance and hop with me:
Take a little dance and hop in the corner—
Hi diddle um dum dee.

Take a little hop and dance with your partner
Take a little hop and dance with me:
Take a little hop and dance with your partner—
Hi diddle um dum dee.

Here comes the blue bird through my window
Here comes the blue bird through my door:
Here comes the blue bird through my window—
Hi diddle um dum dee.

The players stand in a circle with their hands linked and arched high for doors and windows. One girl (the Blue Bird) weaves in and out of these (first verse). The second and third verses are alternative versions of the next action which is to choose a partner from the ring and dance round with her. The girl chosen becomes the new Blue Bird. This game is passing out of favour. At one time birds of all colours were sung of, depending on the colour of the chosen partner's frock, so that her verse might start off, "Here comes the green bird through my window," or "red bird," or "white bird . . ."

Tea without Sugar

✧ I can take my tea without
Sugar, sugar:
I can take my tea without
S U G A R.

S U G A R
S U G A R
I can take my tea without
S U G A R

The girl who's het goes into the middle of the ring which joins hands and begins to circle as the rhyme starts. This centre girl stands quite still until the last "S U G A R," which she spells out on the circling girls. The one on whom the last letter "R" falls then goes into the middle for the next game. In some streets the girl who's het goes round outside the ring of circling players, and she spells out the last "S U G A R" on their backs.

Adree, Adree, I Dropped it

✧　I sent a letter to my love
　And on the way I dropped it:
　Someone must have picked it up
　And put it in their pocket—
　A-dree a-dree a-dree
　A-dree a-dree a-dree
　I dropped it.

All sit in a circle on ground and the one that's out (as the singing begins) goes round the outside of the circle with a hopping step —and a hanky in her hand. This hanky she drops behind someone's back as the verse ends. And whoever discovers it has to chase the dropper. If she's caught, she's out again. If she gets to the empty place in the circle, the other is het. The chaser must follow same path as the dropper, otherwise she's out. This game has other names such as "Codfish" or "Dog and Bone."

Salomé

✧　I'm Shirley Temple and I've got curly hair
　I've got blue eyes and wear my skirts up there:
　I'm no able to do the Betty Grable
　I'm Shirley Temple and I've got curly hair!

　Salomé, Salomé, you should see Salomé
　Hands up there, skirts down there—
　You should see Salomé!

The players join hands and go round in a circle, one girl in the middle. She carries out the following actions:

Line 1: Touches hair.

Line 2: Touches eyes and pulls up skirts.

Line 3: Stops opposite ring player.

Line 4: Touches hair again.

Line 5: She birls round arm in arm with the player.

Line 6: The pair of them raise arms and pull up skirts.

Line 7: They go round arm in arm.

The player chosen from the ring now stays in the middle for the next game.

The Dusting Bluebells

✧ In and out the dusting bluebells
In and out the dusting bluebells
In and out the dusting bluebells
I am your master!

Pitter-pitter-patter on your shoulder
Pitter-pitter-patter on your shoulder
Pitter-pitter-patter on your shoulder
I am your master!

Players join hands in a ring and hold their arms arched high. One girl who has been picked stands in the centre; then, when the singing starts, she begins to go round the circle of girls, weaving in and out the arches. When the second verse is reached, she stops behind one of the girls and pitter-patters with her fingers on her shoulders. As soon as this verse ends, the two girls start off weaving in and out "the dusting bluebells," until the time comes for them to stop behind a third girl for pitter-pattering. This goes on until all the players have joined up in a pitter-pattering train for the last girl; and then, led by her, the train weaves hither and thither, coming eventually to a sudden stop, when someone usually shouts out "London!"

Mary Had a Little Lamb

✧ Mary had a little lamb
She also had a pig,
She sat it on the mantelpiece
To do the Irish jig:
O E-I E-I E-I O
E-I E-I O,
O E-I E-I E-I O
E-I E-I O!

The players join hands and go round girl in middle of ring. During the singing of the first verse, the girl waves her hands up and down. At the word "jig" she stops opposite one of the ring girls. During the "E-I O" chorus, she goes round arm in arm with this girl; and she does the same with the girl directly opposite, so that the three trace out a figure of eight. The first girl chosen from the ring now stands in the centre for the next game.

I Can Do the Rumba

✧ Mary had a little lamb
She sat it on the bunker:
Pretty Polly came along
And made it do the rumba—
I I I I
I can do the rumba:
I I I I
I can do the rumba.

This game is very similar to the previous one, only the girl in the centre does a rumba sort of dance for the verse, and during the chorus she does a rumba with the chosen girl and also with the girl directly opposite.

O alla-tinka

✧ O alla-tinka to do the rumba
O alla-tinka do the
Rumba-umba-umba-umba ay!

I paula-tay paula-tuska
Paula-tay paula-toe:
I paula-tay paula-tuska
Paula-tay paula-toe.

O alla-tinka to do the rumba
O alla-tinka do the
Rumba-umba-umba-umba ay!

Players circle round for first three lines, then girl in centre begins the "I paula-tay paula-tuska" to a sort of jig-step, then at "O alla-tinka" she does a kind of rumba opposite another person, who goes into the centre for the next game.

The Lady on the Mountain

✧ On the mountain stands a lady
Who she is I cannot tell
All she wants in gold and silver
All she wants is a nice young man:

So call in my Davie dear
Davie dear, Davie dear
So call in my Davie dear
Davie dear!

Give her a kiss and a one two three
A one two three, a one two three
Give her a kiss and a one two three
My bonnie dear!

This is a skipping-song, and a ring-game, too. The girls maintain that the boys often join in ring-games—at least, in this one. After Davie's called in, the pair kiss and "do a switch"—that is, cross hands and birl round. The game starts again with Davie calling in some girl from the ring.

Ring-a-Ring-a-Roses

❖ Ring-a-ring-a-roses
A pocketful of posies:
Husha husha
We all fall down.

Down down
In the deep blue sea
Catching tiddlers for my tea—
With a one and a two and a three!

This is the simplest ring-game, played only by very young children. On the last line of the first verse all crouch down. On the last line of the second verse they rise to their feet. Another version goes:

A-ring-a-ring-a-roses
Three black noses
A-choo! A-choo! A-choo!

The Little Sandy Girl

❖ There's a little sandy girl sitting on a stone
Crying, weeping, all the day alone:
Rise up, sandy girl, wipe your tears away
And choose the one that you love best
And then run away!

A very simple ring-game, but most popular. A girl kneels in centre of circling ring. At the line "Crying, weeping . . ." she puts her hands up to her face, then on the next line rises, smiles, and chooses the next "sandy girl," while she goes round in the ring with the others.

The Galley Ship

◇ Three times round went the galley galley ship
And three times round went she,
And three times round went the galley, galley ship
Till she sank to the bottom of the sea.

"Pull 'er up, pull 'er up," cried the little sailor boy
"Pull 'er up, pull 'er up," cried he,
"Pull 'er up, pull 'er up," cried the little sailor boy
But she sank to the bottom of the sea.

Some players use the first verse only. They go round hand in
hand, start "sinking" on the last line, going right down at the
word "sea." They then rise, repeat this last line and its action
until they have done it three times in all. Other players bring
in the second verse after the first when they pull each other up
again and circle round once more before finally sinking.

Punchinello

◇ What can ye do, Punchinello,
Little fellow?
What can ye do, Punchinello,
Little dear?

I can do this, Punchinello,
Little fellow!
I can do this, Punchinello,
Little dear!

We'll do it too, Punchinello,
Little fellow!
We'll do it too, Punchinello,
Little dear!

Who's doing it best, Punchinello,
Little fellow?
Who's doing it best, Punchinello,
Little dear?

You're doing it best, Punchinello,
Little fellow:
You're doing it best, Punchinello,
Little dear!

Verse 1: The players join hands and circle round Punchinello,
who skips and dances in the centre. *Verse* 2: Then perhaps "he"

M

goes down on his "hunkers [hams]" and does a dance like a Russian Cossack, shooting out his legs while the ring goes round. *Verse 3*: The players continue to circle round, singing "We'll do it too . . ." *Verse 4*: The ring halts and each player repeats Punchinello's dance. *Verse 5*: Punchinello points to the best performer, and this player takes Punchinello's place in the middle of the ring. The game goes on with each new Punchinello trying a fresh and (if possible) more daring type of dance.

The Hokey Pokey

• You put your right leg in
You put your right leg out
You put your right leg in
And shake it all about.

You do the hokey pokey
And you turn yourself around
That's what it's all about—See!

O . . . the hokey pokey!
O . . . the hokey pokey!
O . . . the hokey pokey
That's what it's all about—See!

The players form a ring and go round more or less following the instructions of the first two verses. At "—See!" they all stamp their feet. For the three lines "O . . . the hokey pokey!" they stop, stretch out their arms full length, and, after lifting them high over their heads, they sweep them down to the ground and back again. After "—See!" a quick birl follows with another stamp of the foot.

Bonny Jenny

• An old game played sometimes in a row and sometimes in a ring.

Where shall bonny Jenny lie
Jenny lie, Jenny lie?
Where shall bonny Jenny lie
On the co-cold nights of winter?

She shall lie on Katie's bosom
Katie's bosom, Katie's bosom:
She shall lie on Katie's bosom
On the co-cold nights of winter.

The Girl of the Golden City

⬧ The wind, the wind, the wind blows high
The snow comes falling from the sky:
Maisie Drummond says she'll die
For the want of the golden city.

She is handsome, she is pretty
She is the girl of the golden city:
She is handsome, one two three,
Come and tell me who shall be!

R is his first name
His first name, his first name:
R is his first name—
E-I-O, sir!

S is his second name
His second name, his second name:
S is his second name—
E-I-O, sir!

Robert Sinclair is his name
Is his name, is his name:
Robert Sinclair is his name—
E-I-O, sir!

Now's the time to hide your face
Hide your face, hide your face:
Now's the time to hide your face—
E-I-O, sir!

Now's the time to show your face
Show your face, show your face:
Now's the time to show your face
E-I-O, sir!

Now's the time to choose the one
Choose the one, choose the one:
Now's the time to choose the one
E-I-O, sir!

The wind, the wind, the wind blows high
The snow comes falling from the sky:
Libby Cooper says she'll die
For the want of the golden city. . . .

Maisie Drummond stands in the middle of the ring as the rest circle round to the first two verses. At "Come and tell me who shall be," the ring slows down for a passing and whispered consultation which settles that "*R*" is his first name and that "*S*" is his second name. At the next verse, Robert Sinclair's name is announced with a stamp of the foot by each player in the ring. During the sixth verse, Maisie hides her face in her hands, and in the next verse shows herself smiling. The last verse chooses the girl who's next to be in the centre, namely Libby Cooper, and the game goes on. For the line "*R* is his first name," a few streets prefer to say "*R* is his first initial," and instead of "Now's the time to choose the one," "Now's the time to pick a body."

No ring-game is played so much. The music of the introductory verses is rather attractive; and, no matter how often they change from street to street, the words always seem to retain some element of poetry. The line that's most varied is "The want of the golden city," in place of which you may hear:

> . . . The love of the golden city . . .

> . . . The one of the golden city. . . .

> . . . For the love of the boy with the rolling eye. . . .

> . . . If she doesn't get the one with the rainbow tie. . . .

—or ". . . the golden tie," ". . . the tartan tie."

The on-looker or the passer-by overhearing the rumours of this golden city must stop to think back, or to ask and wonder what it all means. Children, thank goodness, never try to explain their poetry. It's the art of play that inspires them: in their dancing, in their singing and in their choice of words. Stevenson said of young people, very wisely: "Surely they dwell in a mythological epoch and are not the contemporaries of their parents." So the golden city (which isn't to be found on any map) may be some eternal capital where time is everlasting. Nevertheless, even in a game like this, children show up as cunning realists. For sometimes they sing:

> She is pretty, she is ugly
> She is one of the ugly sisters . . .

Or:

> She is ugly, she is pretty
> She is the witch of the tin-can city . . .

And, after all, it's in the old industrial maze, it's in this tin-can city that many of us playing as children enjoyed the most glorious visions. When the summer days dragged by like dynasties of Egypt, when the sun and shadow sides of the street eyed each other for a millennium! When beyond such an immense present lay the unbelievable future:

> She is handsome, one two three
> Come and tell me who shall be?

TUNES

All the tunes contained in this appendix were noted down by Andrew D. Miller and transcribed by Robert Crawford.

Bonnie Wee Jeanie

Chinese Government

Down to the Baker's Shop

Have You any Bread and Wine?

How Many Miles to Babylon?

I Ula-used to Li-li-live in Yalla-lankie, Shalla-lankie

I'm a Little Orphan Girl

I'm the Monster of Loch Ness

Mrs Wright

O Me Goss Me Goss Me Golly

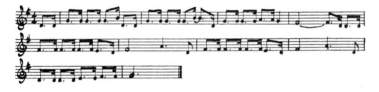

On the Mountain Stands a Lady

One Two Three a-Leerie

Poor Tommy is Dead and Laid in his Grave

Queen Alexandra has Lost her Gold Ring

Rabbie Burns was Born in Ayr

See the Robbers Passing By

The Eely-Alley-O

The Golden City

There Came Three Jews

Water, Water, Wallflower

What Can you Do, Punchinello?

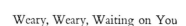

Weary, Weary, Waiting on You

INDEX OF FIRST LINES